INTO THE GREAT
SOLITUDE

BY THE SAME AUTHOR

Against Straight Lines

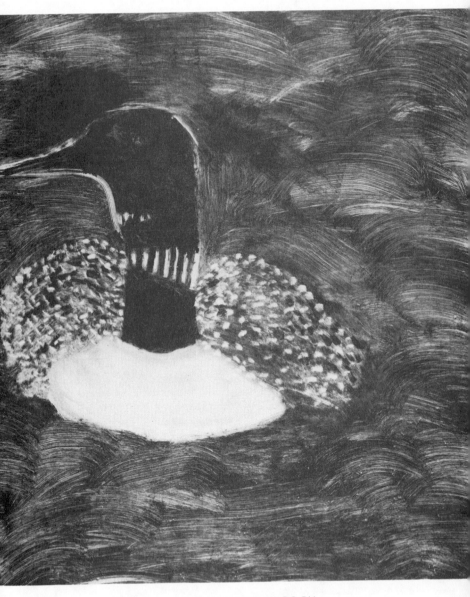

A DONALD HUTTER BOOK
HENRY HOLT AND COMPANY   NEW YORK

INTO THE GREAT
SOLITUDE

AN ARCTIC JOURNEY

ROBERT PERKINS

Published by Henry Holt and Company, Inc.,
115 West 18th Street, New York, New York 10011.
Published in Canada by Fitzhenry & Whiteside Limited,
195 Allstate Parkway, Markham, Ontario L3R 4T8.

Library of Congress Cataloging-in-Publication Data
Perkins, Robert
Into the great solitude: an Arctic journey / by Robert Perkins. —
1st ed.
p.   cm.
"A Donald Hutter book."
1. Back River (N.W.T.)—Description and travel.   2. Canoes and
canoeing—Northwest Territories—Back River.   3. Back River Valley
(N.W.T.)—Description and travel.   4. Perkins, Robert—Journeys—
Northwest Territories—Back River.   I. Title.
F1100.B33P46   1991
917.19'4—dc20   90-44465
CIP

Henry Holt books are available at special discounts
for bulk purchases for sales promotions, premiums,
fund-raising, or educational use. Special editions
or book excerpts can also be created to specification.
For details contact:
Special Sales Director, Henry Holt and Company, Inc.,
115 West 18th Street, New York, New York 10011

FIRST EDITION

Book design by Claire Naylon Vaccaro
Map by Claudia Carlson
Photos by Susanne Lingemann
Monoprints and line drawings by the author
Printed in the United States of America
Recognizing the importance of preserving
the written word, Henry Holt and Company, Inc.,
by policy, prints all of its first editions
on acid-free paper. ∞

1 3 5 7 9 10 8 6 4 2

Grateful acknowledgment is made to The Charles E. Tuttle Company, Inc., of Rutland, Vermont, and
Tokyo, Japan, for permission to reprint from Narrative of the Arctic Land Expedition to the
Mouth of the Great Fish River, 1833, 1834, and 1835 by George Back, republished in 1970.

To Nick Shields
1950–1971

If only we arrange our life according to that principle which counsels us that we must always hold to the difficult, then that which now still seems to us the most alien will become what we most trust and find faithful.

—Rainer Maria Rilke, *Letters to a Young Poet*

ACKNOWLEDGMENTS

Grateful acknowledgment is made to the 150 individuals who helped make the expedition possible, and to Echo Bay Mines, Inc., for its sponsorship of the Public Broadcasting System film, especially to its president, John Zigarlick, its chairman, Robert F. Calman, and the men and women at the Luplin mine.

Although I am unable to thank everyone, there are a few whose contributions, financial and otherwise, made the difference between success and failure: William Ackerly; Marshall Agnew; Alexander Anderson; William N. Banks; Petty Benitz; Upton Bradey; Barbara Bromley; Megan Cairns; Derek Curtis; Jim Curtis; William Desmond; Charlene Engelhard; Bruce Fader; David Fanning; Francis Forbes; Henry W. Fuller; David M. Grose; Bayard and Julie Henry; George C. Hixon; Elise Hull; Charles W. Jefferson; Tony and Judy King; Fred Levy; C. Douglas Lewis III; Sandy A. Mactaggart; James Merrill; Andrew Paneyko; Evelyn M. Perkins; Thomas H. Perkins; Sam Plimpton; Ann

Rippon; David Rockefeller, Jr.; Pete and Jean Shields; Sandi Simon; Fred and Marjorie Stockwell; Davis Taylor; Allan Vaughan; Michael Winston; Jacob C. Wolterbeck; Elsie P. Youngman; William S. Youngman.

Several companies generously contributed equipment or expertise to the expedition: Earthwatch, The Explorers Club, J. M. Forbes & Co., Harvard Travelers Club, Soul-Joy in Body-Fort Natural Foods, Water Survey of Canada, Wilderness Canoe Association.

The film was made by The New Film Company and shown on the PBS *Adventure* series created by WGBH, Boston. Susanne Lingemann traveled with the film crew and took the still photographs.

The manuscript was brought from a rough journal to legibility by the word processing wizardry of Sylvia Camp, Fred Levy, Ari Kreith, and David Merson. Sylvia deserves extra thanks for having the courage to decipher the original journal's handwriting.

I will forever be indebted to Denny Alsop and *Loon*, the canoe he built.

I would like to thank The Explorers Club for allowing me to carry a Club flag. Each flag, and there are many, has a card stating who carried it and on what expedition. I had hoped to find one from an Arctic expedition, but the early flags of Cook and Peary have been retired. Instead, I carried the flag that Thor Heyerdahl took on his journey in *Ra*. Not having a mast to fly it from, I used it as a pillow.

Several people generously gave of their time to read and comment on the manuscript. The finished book has been enhanced by their honesty: Audie, David Belknap, Alexandra and Garrett Conover, David Conover, Roger F. Pasquier, Beekman H. Pool, Elizabeth Pool, Mary van Roden, Laurie Weisz, and Kit White and Andrea Barnet.

My editor, Donald Hutter, made writing the book a reality.

Because of his faith and encouragement, the book was born. His presence is sorely missed but his memory is an inspiration. And my thanks to Amy Hertz, who is now my editor, and to Claire Naylon Vaccaro, who has designed this handsome book.

An Arctic Journey

An Exploration
in Solitude
Down the
Back River

0 10 20 30 40 50 60
Miles

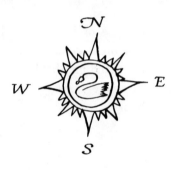

N

W E

S

THE BAR

Beechey Lake

Beechey Portage

White Wolf

Willows

Esker Valley

PERKINS'S
BEGINNING

Malley's Rapids

Muskox Lake

Sussex Lake

Aylmer
Lake

©Claudia Carlson

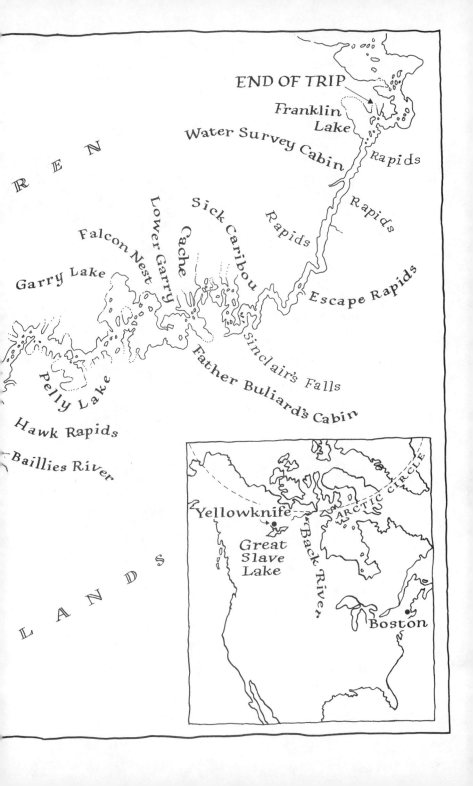

True wisdom is only found far away from people, out in the great solitude, and it is not found in play but only through suffering. Solitude and suffering open the human mind, and therefore a shaman must seek his wisdom there.

—Recorded by Greenland ethnographer Knud Rasmussen during his Fifth Thule Expedition from Greenland to Siberia, 1921–1924

I.

SURELY THE LOON IS A CURIOUS CREATURE

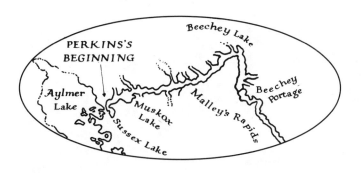

JUNE 21–JULY 23, 1987

To *travel alone* is risky business, especially into a wilderness; equally risky is to have dreams and not follow them. The risks I perceive, standing on the dock in Yellowknife, are palpable: during the next ten weeks, canoeing on a remote Arctic river, I might throw my back out, break a leg, lose my canoe, get lost, or simply drown. Although these thoughts scare me, I remind myself that far to the south exists another world, equally hazardous but harder to visualize. There are many kinds of wilderness, not just this indifferent treeless tundra north of me. Facing the summer and all its unknowns, I consider myself lucky compared to some people back home.

White fluffy clouds are sailing over Yellowknife from the northwest: a perfect day for flying. My planning is over. The fund-raising and the packing are behind me. I have driven three thousand miles, not across America, but northwest from Boston, along the Trans-Canada Highway, north to Edmonton, Alberta, then due north from there to the end of the road in Yellowknife.

Open an atlas to the map of North America or, better yet, to northern Canada, and let your eye find the landmass between Alaska and Hudson Bay called the Northwest Territories. Toward the center of this space you'll see a large lake in the shape of a swan in flight, Great Slave Lake. North of the northeast corner of the lake are a chain of smaller lakes: Artillery, Clinton-Colden, and Aylmer. These lakes lead to the headwaters of the Back River, a river that flows across the top of the Territories in a northeasterly direction until it reaches the Arctic Ocean at the foot of Chantrey Inlet. The Back is the king and queen of Arctic rivers: long, tough, beautiful, dangerous, and magnificent to canoe. The wildness, the romance, the history, and the adventure of this river— the longest North American river entirely embraced by the tundra—have drawn me here. I don't expect to see anyone. There are no settlements between where I will be dropped off and the place where I will be picked up on the Arctic coast. At the mouth of the river is a sport fishing camp, but by the time I arrive there in late August, the camp will be closed, winter will have begun. No Eskimos, or, as they prefer to be called, Inuit, live in the interior. The government moved the last families out in the 1950s because they were starving. Never mind that for centuries they had managed to live off this land and called it their home. My world, the world of commerce and progress and soul saving, corrupted the Inuit and undermined their culture. Now this vast land supports nothing but itself, its animals, its flora, fish, birds, and weather.

I stand on the dock watching the clouds as the pilot and base manager run the last checks on the float plane after loading my few pieces of equipment. The canoe is lashed tight to the struts of the starboard float. A shiver of excitement—or fear— flows through me. I stand on the edge of a great adventure, the realization of a dream only one person thought would ever occur.

A piece of dream became my touchstone all winter. It had

to do with loons, a bad night's sleep, and snow. "Surely the loon is a curious creature," I scribbled while half asleep. I named my canoe after the dream, after the loon. There she is in the sunlight: slim, small, and handsome, painted black and white, yin and yang, like the colors of her namesake, the oldest bird listed in the field guide. During the spring, few people who saw *Loon* appreciated the unusual canoe my friend Denny Alsop was building. She doesn't resemble a traditional canoe. Remarks were made about whether she would float. To many she seemed to be

an ugly duckling and not the wonderful canoe Denny and I knew her to be. Her sides curve in toward the centerline; there is no rise in the bow or the stern. She looks delicate, but isn't. "Surely the loon is a curious creature." Like any dream, mine seemed to have arrived from nowhere, but it stuck, acting as an interior lightning rod for something equally implausible: this trip.

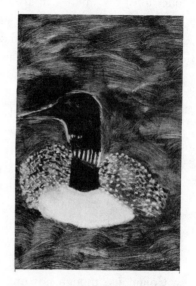

Watching the flight crew prepare the small plane, I think of my father in a Boston hospital room. Earlier this spring, a standard operation on his seventy-two-year-old heart created unusual complications. Two days after my departure for Yellowknife, he collapsed. He didn't realize that while he was recuperating, he was bleeding internally. My mother told me on the phone this morning that if the doctors can find the leak and make his blood clot, they give him a fifty-fifty chance. This is harder on her than on him. He has only to fight for his life. She has to watch and worry. "He might die" wasn't on anyone's lips during the spring, but it was on our minds.

As the operation approached, he sent his five children an article from a medical journal describing the upcoming surgery. It did not mention complications. In my hectic rush to complete my preparations I ignored it, and the operation, choosing instead to believe, as he said, that this was no big deal.

Between us exists a host of sparring, competitive feelings. If a healthy relationship includes adversity, ours is robust.

My father has never shown much enthusiasm for the direction my life has taken. He worries about my risk-taking, my questions, my interest in art—all of which have never earned a penny. His world revolves around finances and dividends, annual reports and newspapers. I find community in wilderness; he finds his in wife, friends, sailing, and *The Wall Street Journal*. He's interested in order; I'm not—not that kind, anyway.

Five minutes before the plane takes off. Five minutes to think of what I've forgotten, what else I need. I can't shake the thought of my father lying in that white room. This morning on the phone my mother sounded tired; her voice said there was no change in his condition. That's it for the summer: no change. That's all I'll know until I come out: a fifty-fifty chance, and no change.

Our family grew up by the sea, and we spent the time my father had for us on the sea. We've learned to accept, as has our mother, that the sea is the object of his deepest affection. He is a Columbus, though not one venturing forth to discover New Worlds. He likes gunkholing downeast, poking in and out of known and unknown anchorages. He's owned two boats: *Puffin* and, for the last twenty-seven years, *Goldeneye*, a Concordia yawl, by modern standards an old-fashioned wooden yacht, graceful but definitely old-fashioned. This suits him fine. He couldn't care less about modern designs.

During the summer he'd as soon sit on *Goldeneye* tied up to the dock as be anywhere. Winters he'd stay put by his fire, enjoy his family, and putter on boat-related tasks, read navigation books, and dream about next summer's cruising. Even by Boston standards, he's considered old-fashioned.

He came home from work one night, years ago, and announced to my mother that they would go on a winter vacation. They never took winter vacations. That was time taken away from summer sailing.

She didn't believe him. She had never been to Europe, let alone to the tropics in winter. But while she prepared dinner and he went to change clothes, her suspicion warmed to enthusiasm. She imagined them walking on endless stretches of white beach, with palm trees, heat, a turquoise sea, more heat, and moonlit dinners. As a native Californian, she easily saw herself out of the slush, the cold, and the depressing gray skies of Massachusetts. She was imagining what she'd pack when he reappeared, ready to make them cocktails. She asked him which island they were going to.

"Island?" he said quizzically. "I've reserved a room at the Ritz in town, an island of sorts. I thought it would be fun to spend a week there." Mistaking my mother's look of disappointment for one of disapproval, he said apologetically, "We could go to a less expensive hotel, but look at it this way: I can go to the office every day; you'll be near your friends, and besides, why would anyone want to go to someplace where they didn't know your name?"

The plane has no difficulty lifting off the water with my light load. The pilot, Larry, remarks on how little drag my canoe makes as he banks the plane and circles the town before heading northeast out over Great Slave Lake. Below us, Latham Island, known as Old Town, is dotted with handsome homes, many with docks extending out into the water like rectangular tongues. Small sailboats are tied to them or anchored nearby. This is a far cry from the Yellowknife of the old days. Then the town had more dreams than residents, more tents than houses. Time, several gold mines, and the arrival of the Territorial government changed all that. Today Yellowknife has high-rise buildings, gourmet food shops, hot tubs, and fresh-cut flowers flown in from the south.

Yellowknife is a boomtown, the administrative center for the whole Northwest Territory, a landmass larger than India. There aren't 50,000 people in the whole area. Since 1967, when the new commissioner of the NWT, Stewart Hodgson, stepped onto the red carpet from his plane, the town's population has tripled to 15,000 people. Like scavengers, all the ills of larger cities have found homes here too: pollution, discrimination, over-development, poor zoning, alcoholism, drugs. It is an island of human restlessness in a sea of wilderness. Five hundred miles of dirt-and-gravel road connect it to the south. It's easier to fly here than to drive. Most of its people come from somewhere else, yet the town is self-contained, and acts it, set apart by its isolation and its long winter months of almost complete darkness.

From the air, Yellowknife resembles a ship frozen into an ocean of land. Most passengers on this ship go to the railing, to the edge of town. I can see a slim tracery of roads reaching out but as Larry levels the plane, they soon peter out. I discern one road, hidden in the spruce trees, from the dust following the progress of a truck. What seemed a dense forest of spruce from the ground now looks sparse, the way my thinning hair appears fuller when I look straight into a mirror.

Below the plane, the last tag ends of civilization begin to drop away: no more roads, no houses, no fuel caches. We seem suspended immobile in the sky, with the earth turning under us. The number of trees diminishes until there are none left below or ahead of us. We have entered the barren ground, or tundra, where a myriad of lakes and ponds sparkle in the landscape. Their shapes resemble the pieces of a giant's jigsaw puzzle absently scattered around.

While the plane's engine hums away, I smile as I look at the landscape and remember the day, in 1975, when I discovered the Back River existed. My first job after college was in the art department at a library called the Boston Athenaeum. As I poked about in the northern history section, in my gray librarian's smock, my eyes fell on a fat volume entitled *Narrative of the Arctic Land Expedition to the Mouth of the Great Fish River, 1833, 1834, and 1835,* by an Englishman, George Back, captain in the Royal Navy. I stood there most of the afternoon reading his journal.

Finding that volume sparked my first journey into the barrens. The following summer, 1976, Bernie Peyton, a college roommate, and I retraced Back's route from the shores of Great Slave Lake to Chantrey Inlet. We paddled an eighteen-foot wood-and-canvas Old Town canoe and carried enough supplies to sink us. We paddled fast, ate a lot, fished a lot, enjoyed each other's company immensely, and couldn't wait to get home.

After our summer in the north, Bernie's life path shifted toward becoming a wildlife biologist. I envied him the clarity of his choice. I share his love for animals and might have gone into some form of natural science, but haven't. As a consequence, I remain intellectually unbaptized, but equally devoted.

Canoeing the Back River is hardly a first, not even for me, because other people—not many, but some—have traveled the length of this river, starting with Captain Back in 1834. This time I am headed to the Back alone.

Larry cuts north. He points ahead to a line on the horizon, to the blink of ice from a frozen lake. What I feared may be true: although today is June 21 and Yellowknife's temperature is 70 degrees, and although the snow has melted off the barrens, the still water of the deep lakes remains frozen. If the lakes leading to the Back River are frozen, I'll have difficulty retracing all of George Back's route. Even if the plane finds open water to land on, do I want to risk traveling on ice? The first summer storms and punky, rotten ice would make it treacherous work. With hand signs, we decide to go on to the first lake, Artillery, and fly north toward the headwaters of the Back River until we find open water.

The day before, in the Latham Island float base, a few of the pilots and mechanics stood around as I went over my itinerary with the base manager, Norm Case. One whole wall of the room is a map of the Territories. A nail holds a string that Norm uses to calculate distances, and prices, from Yellowknife. Colored pins stuck in the map indicate either fixed or summer work camps out on the land. Away from Yellowknife, the pins thin out quickly. There were no pins out toward the Back River. Larry, sitting beside me now in the plane sipping ginger ale, wearing only sneakers and shorts, had asked me what type of gun I was bringing to protect myself from bears. I said I carried a .22. He laughed and the other men in the room picked up their heads.

"However," I said, "M-80 firecrackers are good grizzly bear protection—the sound scares them away. The .22 is only to procure small birds or game for survival." The room went quiet. No one called me a fool, but they all thought it. They had lived in the north too long to trust their lives to the goodwill of the land or of a barren-ground grizzly bear. A high-powered rifle, preferably with hollow-point bullets, is their choice of protection against the unexpected.

The desk sergeant at the Royal Canadian Mounted Police office, where I filed my itinerary, said he hoped the wind wasn't blowing when I tried to light my firecrackers. He told me how bears can kill humans: a quick swat to the head, which breaks your neck, or disembowelment, by hugging you and raking your stomach with the five-inch claws of a hind foot. You can't outrun them. If you're lucky enough, and the bear is only curious, you could play dead while it sniffed or slapped you around. The other Mounties in the room laughed, but not me. I doubted whether I'd have the courage to lie still under the nose of a curious grizzly.

The worst story in the float base was told very matter-of-factly by a pilot named Ron. He'd been flying a helicopter two summers before, resupplying a geology exploration camp where a man and a woman were working. As Ron flew into the camp, a large bear fled from the helicopter's noise. Ron landed fast but did not see anyone until he walked into the camp. He found the woman with both her arms ripped off and massive cuts all over her body. The man lay bleeding and unconscious, with several crushed ribs and a punctured lung. Only through the fluke of Ron's arrival did the couple survive.

I tried to laugh these tales off, saying to myself I was more on the bear's side; that I even supported the right to arm bears instead of bear arms; that these attacks took place at fixed camps; that it was really the people's fault. But deep inside I felt the fear, and today, looking out the plane's window, I feel it rising again. In less than an hour I'll be on my own.

To distract myself, I begin watching the plane's shadow as it ripples over the surface of the lakes and rocks and tundra. Each rise and fall, each fold in the landscape, distorts it. I think of the land's former residents, the Caribou Inuit, whose culture was based on the caribou, not sea mammals, who believed that everything with a shadow was alive. For myself, I think how like the shadow of the float plane my everyday self is: pulled along, altered by each hill, each obstacle, as I struggle to keep up with my higher spirit.

Flying up Artillery, then Clinton-Colden Lake, we find only the narrows of each lake unfrozen. Over the engine noise, Larry says he'll put me down in any open water I want. I'm nervous about the ice. My plan was to become used to *Loon* and the equipment as I paddled up the lakes, taking my time to acclimatize to the tundra. To start in ice would be no help. The snow melted recently; the land is still pale and brown. The willows are in bud. We cross Sandhill Bay on Aylmer Lake, the third lake, and see open water on Sussex Lake, the headwaters of the Back River. By flying here, I save a hundred miles of tobogganing, pulling, and portaging over and around rotten ice.

As the plane begins circling lower, I think of the differences between George Back and someone like myself. The modern advances in technology—airplanes, radios, excellent lightweight equipment from socks to tents—make me a tourist. These first explorers, through their fortitude and perseverance, even in their failures, outshine what now passes for exploration. The geographical unknowns that drew these men on no longer exist. Modern-day explorers are left with adventure and the potential for personal growth. Today discoveries are made under the ocean's surface, in outer space, or under a microscope, and modern Columbuses rely heavily on the aid of technology.

Larry interrupts my thoughts to point out a large blond esker that looks like an incongruous beach backed by a sand dune. Eskers aren't loose sand dunes, but a mixture of rocks, pebbles, and sand. They are the streambeds of glacial rivers, normal in many respects, but they have been deposited on the land as raised ridges, a mirror image of a typical riverbed. They remark the passage of vast amounts of time and glacial activity. An esker's full course is harder to see today. They've been cut into, chopped through by modern rivers, worn away by other earth movement, until fragments like the one I see seem like isolated islands.

Over the engine's roar, I yell, "That's fine." Larry begins his final circle, checking the water depth and looking for rocks. Soon the canoe tied to the struts will be floating. Soon everything will be unloaded. Soon I'll be on my own.

My father's odds of surviving this summer, let alone another year, are no better than fifty-fifty. He's an unusually lucky man, especially when rolling dice in backgammon. Even during the years we had little to say to each other, we continued to play the game. He almost always wins. He says I play too recklessly. How do you beat such a lucky man except by taking chances? This summer both of us will be rolling dice against rough odds across a board as big as heaven.

The land and water grow more distinct in every detail. As the pontoons touch water, the plane rejoins its shadow. We skim along, then slow and settle. Larry turns and taxis the plane to the tongue of the esker. He climbs out, takes a long line with him from inside the cockpit, secures one end to a cleat on the front of the pontoon, and jumps ashore, looking for a big rock to tie the other end around. I climb out. We begin to unload. The sun's glare on the sand makes it very bright. The heat feels good. After unloading, Larry puts on a pair of reflective sunglasses and a pair of navy-blue overalls and walks away from me, up the esker. His dark shape ripples in the heat rising off the sand. He walks with his head down. Returning a few minutes later, he explains, "On these eskers you find things—arrowheads and things. The wind blows away the sand and there they are, just sitting there."

The only unusual thing I notice is a bone of some kind, bleached white in the sun, half buried in the sand.

Larry turns, regards me a moment, and says, "You're lucky. The bugs aren't out." Then he shakes my hand, saying, "Take care. Good-bye." After undoing the line from the rock, he pushes on the pontoon, jumps on it, and climbs into the cockpit. The light breeze drifts the small plane onto the lake. In another minute the engine starts. He taxis down the lake, turns, and, with a gradually increasing roar, races back at me. Gracefully the plane lifts off the water. The silver body circles higher and higher and begins to shrink until it resembles a grain of salt and disappears. With him, Larry takes the noise and the last link with the world I know. In the silence flooding in, I feel my known world begin to break apart on the shore of the tundra, the way the sea at home breaks on the coast.

I move my two packs, the red box, or wannigan, and the two camera cases off the esker to my first campsite near the water. The packs carry most of the food and my personal gear. The wannigan is my kitchen and holds ten days of food. If I eat the food in less than ten days, I have to suffer. I can't afford to go into the large food pack sooner. This stiff wooden box, made of lightweight plywood, glue, and staples, also holds sharp and bulky items, like the frying pan and stove. Carrying them in the wannigan, I don't feel them dig against my back.

As if in a daze, I find the tent. I've practiced, but it's still a new tent and I'm not used to setting it up. Struggling with the fly and tent poles, I get the uneasy feeling I'm being watched. I turn to see a gull. To be exact, a glaucous gull that has flapped out of the sky to watch. The tilt of its head and the look in its eye let me know my attempt to erect the tent strikes it as comical. At the same time it seems to be saying, Why don't you do something useful, like feed me? Asking the gull to leave has no effect. I wave my arms. It flaps back ten feet, as unimpressed with my attempt to fly as it is with my camp skills. I ignore it. Three more join the first one.

With the tent up, I begin other "chores," consisting of either touching everything to be sure it's really here or picking everything up and moving it two feet: the paddles, the wannigan, the food pack, even *Loon*. Finally I begin to settle down. I unroll my personal pack, lay out my sleeping bag, and arrange my extra clothes. I've brought sneakers and a pair of L. L. Bean boots, several pairs of wool and cotton socks, a light and a heavy pair of pants and shirts, some fishnet undershirts and nylon underwear, gloves, rain clothes, and a beautiful anorak made by my sister Eve. I also have seven different hats. I don't know why I carry so many, except changing hats pleases me.

The first afternoon my mind remains a jumble of different thoughts—about my father, what I did to get here, and ancient, nearly forgotten memories. I am curious to see how this much time by myself will reorder, or skew, my world. My desire is to understand more about nature's qualities: to learn her grammar in other ways than the mechanized and scientific one; to dig into her roots, to uncover the Anglo-Saxon, the Sanskrit, the Latin, and the Greek; not to confirm what I've been taught, or been told, or read about her, but to look for myself. Is it an impossible apprenticeship? My mind ventures everywhere but into the present moment.

Growing up, I had a summertime neighbor named Peter, who was seven years older than I. Not having an older brother made it hard to resist falling under his influence. While I was between the ages of eight and twelve, he became an influential teacher, introducing me to another side of nature, a darker side, the world of controlled experiments, investigatory theory, and objective observation of animals. Human participation in what he observed played a large role. His animal experiments made pithing the frog in biology class look like a benign form of animal worship.

One day we went out on his lawn where we dug a hole looking for earthworms. Peter and I carried a syringe and a glass of water. Twenty-five earthworms were collected for this experiment. He asked, "What if you pump an earthworm full of air with a syringe? How large in diameter would one be able to expand before exploding? What if you perforated the worm with numerous holes as you pumped him up, then released one full syringe of water into the bloated body? Would the worm resemble the green lawn hose whose perforations sprout numerous tiny jets of water?" Yes, the poor worms did.

I was both drawn to him and scared. There was target practice on baby birds in their nests, and on goldfish in a small pond, as well as endless paper targets. The fish upset me most. I came to this pond in the woods a lot. I used to sit by its edge, watching the shapes and orange color of the few carp appear at the surface. The two black carp were hard to see, but you could if you tried. When I first sat down, nothing would be visible. But slowly they would rise again to caress the water's surface. That's when Peter would shoot them.

Once I stood at ten paces with an apple on my head. He assured me he wouldn't miss, and he didn't. Another year Peter would have me swing a bat lure at twilight out in a field. As the

high-pitched whistle attracted bats, he began his experiment to see if they could fly through the pattern of pellets from a .16-gauge shotgun. Many couldn't.

On the last day I saw him we went to Beverly and bought a pistol. He was nineteen now, a graduate of marine boot camp and trained to kill. Seeing him in uniform, I was once again completely won over. I wanted nothing more than to become like him. We had a date after my next day's summer camp to try the new pistol, but when the time came, he wasn't around. I couldn't find him. That evening my father gathered us around the kitchen table to say Peter was dead. He'd shot himself. For years afterward I asked myself other "what ifs" about Peter's final experiment. What if I had been with him?

I haven't thought of Peter in a long time. This must be part of adjusting to the tundra, to being alone. I pack and repack and shuffle my bits and pieces around. One thing is clear: I've brought too much.

¤   ¤   ¤

An older native I know, born in the tundra, once described to me how he traveled as a young man. At that time, his family lived near the confluence of the Contwoyto and the Back rivers. Other families were sprinkled throughout the huge area. He and his two dogs, Butcher and Brownie, each carrying a small pack, would set off each summer to go "visiting." All he carried was his gun. He really liked July, he said. I asked him what he did about the bugs, because the black flies can be severe in mid-July. He looked at me and said, "What bugs?" I asked where he slept at night. He said, "I'd crawl under a rock." I'm sure he did. I have too much with me. I have to learn to let go.

I carry a plastic pink flamingo, actually half of one. At home people use them as lawn decorations. Here it makes me smile every time I see it, especially if I've been away from camp for a day. Another seemingly unnecessary item is my kalimba. This African thumb piano is my music. I play it by plucking at the thin metal bars attached across the top of a small wooden box. It makes a friendly sound in such immense space.

The food weighs more than anything else. Everyone's relationship to camp food differs but falls somewhere between two schools of thought: Food as Fuel and Food as Ritual. Each one works.

The Food as Fuel advocates prize efficiency and speed. They premix and prepackage and use a lot of expensive, but lightweight, freeze-dried food, which is easy to prepare: just add water. To compensate for its deficiencies, many freeze-dried food makers restore mystery to the meal by unwittingly including a game with each package called "Guess how many people this meal really feeds." It's never as many people as the package lists.

The other group treats food as a ritual and derives pleasure from preparing meals. They enjoy soaking, cutting, mixing, measuring, and even baking from scratch. Many go so far as to grow their own vegetables and dry them in the sun, or in an oven.

Some prepare their own jerky. Whole grains, sharp cheddar cheese, split peas and lentils, dried fruit, flour, and baking powder or yeast are what they bring. Over the next months, there will be a lot of meals for me to cook, and preparation will be part of their enjoyment.

The cameras are unnecessary equipment. I don't like television and have never used cameras or wanted to. Yet I am carrying fifty pounds of Super-8 movie camera equipment in two watertight cases. One Pelican case has 110 rolls of film and the other holds three Super-8 cameras, extra batteries, and sound equipment.

In meeting Chris Knight some months earlier I had found a filmmaker convinced of the positive power of good television. I was standing in the middle of his hectic office describing my trip. Not halfway through, he excused himself and returned with one of the two Pelican cases I have with me. He set it on the floor at my feet.

"Can you carry that in your canoe?" he asked. I bent down and picked it up easily. There was nothing in it.

"Sure," I said.

"Good. That's all you'll need to make a PBS special." Then he told me what that PBS special cost and I nearly fell over.

"Chris, I haven't even raised the money for the trip, let alone anything extra for filming it!"

"Well, okay. Maybe not a PBS special. Maybe just a film," he said, and quoted a smaller, but still large, figure that was higher than the cost of my entire trip.

But Chris was convincing. By April, a month before leaving, I had raised enough money to cover my trip plus the smaller filming figure. Because of our hectic schedules, I received an hour of instruction from Chris on how to make a film.

Always the optimist, he said, "Don't worry. I'll write you some good instructions. You'll have plenty of time to study them up there."

The first time we put the camera on the canoe and the canoe in Boston's Charles River, he forgot to secure the onboard tripod. Underway, the camera and tripod first teetered, then fell slowly into the water. I've never seen him move faster.

He caught the tripod's leg as it sank. He held the camera up to let the water drain out and said, pointing to the camera, "Lesson number one, Rob. Don't do that. Cameras don't like it and neither do I."

In agreeing to make a film, I've created a dilemma. Let's say I succeed and make a good film, a film that tells a personal story about the three points on the tundra triangle: land, animals, and people. Do I run the risk of exposing the tundra to the curiosity of many people? Instead of accomplishing something positive for what I love, will I have achieved the opposite? Several acquaintances said as much. To them, long trips are undertaken quietly, not talked about, and never presented to the public. However, there is little time remaining before what Thoreau called "the preservation of the world" is used up, gone. Only through helping change people's attitudes is there hope of preserving wilderness.

To complement my filming and ensure some good footage, Chris suggested he join me for a few days near the trip's beginning and again at the end. He wanted to film me as if the landscape were looking at me, so the film wouldn't be completely from my point of view. He felt the mixture of the two would allow an audience to understand the magnitude of my undertaking. We picked a point on the map, at the foot of Muskox Lake, where Chris and his crew of three will join me for four days. To reach this spot, I will have been traveling twenty days. After they fly away, I will have fifty days of traveling, the rest of the short Arctic summer, to reach my destination. The gamble is that nothing happens to slow me down. I need to make my rendezvous at Muskox Lake and at the end of the river. If I'm held up, the plane will fly the river the day it arrives to search for me. Low fuel and uncertain weather will limit the extent and effectiveness of this initial search. If the Royal Canadian Mounted Police are called in, I'll be officially lost. I'd never want that. If I'm hurt and unable to signal the plane, the odds of their finding me are poor. As effective as carrying an Emergency Locator Transmitter can be, I'd have to have it near me to use it. What if I tip over and lose all my gear, along with the ELT? What if I break my leg ten miles inland from camp, ten miles from the ELT? I can hear Peter say, "What if . . . ?"

Meeting the film crew will seem like a reunion: Chris, the photographer Susanne Lingemann, and the sound man, *Loon*'s creator, Denny Alsop. The fourth film crew member will be Beekman Pool, a puckish seventy-eight-year-old friend and northern scholar who jumped for joy to make another excursion into the Arctic. His first trip to Labrador in 1930 was followed by many more, but it's been in his study of the north—Inuit culture, art, and the journals of travelers and missionaries and scientists— that he's traveled farthest through the Arctic.

I will spend several days at this first camp. As I had planned to paddle up the three big lakes, getting used to *Loon* and the tundra, I am ten days ahead of myself.

On the third afternoon I set up the tripod and camera. I want to film wildlife, but the only thing that qualifies as wildlife is the gull that parades back and forth on the thin strip of beach in front of the tent, basking in the attention I show it. Instead, I go for a walk with the small, hand-held, wide-angle camera, the Nigra. Of the three cameras, Chris says this is the most indestructible. I film two small bird's nests in the alders. The clusters of eggs and the fresh grass nests lined with feathers make me realize that June is still early spring here.

I'd like to say my love of animals, wilderness, and woodcraft comes from being brought up in a wolf den after the tragic death of both parents in a boating accident in the north; but I can't. I grew up in a ho-hum world around Boston, not more than a stone's throw from Walden Pond, the Battle of Lexington, and Salem where they hanged witches. It's a world full of human history. People are more interested in their own soap operas than they are in what Mother Nature's up to. But even hidden in the suburbs, a multitude of worlds exist, alive with small animals and birds.

The birds always held me spellbound.

Before we moved to Manchester to be near the ocean, we lived in Needham. The second floor of this house had a living room with large picture windows facing north and south. I was often plunked down by our Scottish nurse, Miss MacLeod, to play on that floor. I could see out each side of the house. One afternoon, turning from my wooden blocks to the window, my nose touching the cool glass, I heard a thump. Instantly, as if by magic, a powdery impression of two wings and a small body appeared on the glass inches in front of my face. Terrified, I screamed. In quick succession there were several more thumps. None of the adults rushing in could fathom what had scared me. Too young to know these were birds, I was old enough to have my own inarticulate interpretation. Because I had not actually seen the bird hit the window, only the instant appearance of its body's after-image, I was convinced, and remained convinced for years, that I'd seen an angel.

My father found the crumpled bodies of the cedar waxwings in the shrubbery below the north window. Because the birds saw through the house, they thought they could fly through it. Instead, they broke their necks. Afterward, to prevent more such miscalculations, my mother kept a blind drawn or a bushy plant on the windowsill. My father kept several of the small, colorful wing feathers to put in the hat band of his fedora. What I've kept is the gossamer image of an unforgiving angel appearing out of thin air, in front of my tiny, terrified face.

The second bird I heard years later in Manchester. My room

was on the second floor. The trees nearest our house were white pines and hemlocks. Especially on late August evenings, a mysterious sound often entered through my open window. Every other kind of neighborhood bird I could picture, but not this night bird. To me, its sound was without body, a call through a black window from another world. The encompassing canopy of pine needles, the thick smell of these trees, amplified the whippoorwill's call, condensing night, causing me to shiver, and snapping to attention the drowsy, silent mysteries lurking in the dark outside my window.

The third bird I heard on Squam Lake in New Hampshire. During a summer visit to my friend Nate, I heard a loon. We might have been ten years old. Like the whippoorwill, I heard this bird before I saw it. Right away I felt these two birds understood silence and darkness and secrets that only they were allowed to speak of. The loon was different from other birds, even from the whippoorwill. I could listen happily to the whippoorwill, but the loon's cry sank into my young soul directly, stirring up and tangling me in feelings and moods I didn't even know I possessed. This sound conveyed mysteries even the whippoorwill hadn't dreamed of.

To me, science stands mute at the threshold where my questions begin. These inarticulate questions, and Nature, slip gracefully between the facts—like a wild animal, whose foreknowledge of your presence allows it to melt quietly away without being perceived.

On top of the esker, I lie down on my back by a big rock to film the view by sighting along my legs and feet. This one is roughly 150 feet high and several hundred yards long. The breeze is strong on top and feels good. The sun's brightness gives the impression of afternoon, although it is closer to 10:00 P.M. The sun won't be low enough to create night until August.

The flat view races to the horizon in all directions. Sussex Lake, the headwater of the Back, still has ice floating on it. From certain angles, the still-solid white ice on Aylmer Lake that I see through a gap in two hills on the other side of Sussex Lake resembles a wall. Many birds have enjoyed a boulder at the northern tip of the esker as a watchtower. I imagine the jaeger, the owl, the falcon, even the gulls using it to scan for prey, or to eat on. Several fine bundles of gray fur and tiny bones, the inedible parts of prey, regurgitated by the owls, lie on the ground by the rock. The white gook on the rock could be from any number of birds. The macaroni-shaped droppings and the round pellets at the rock's base show that the raptors' prey, the ptarmigan and the rabbit, also use the rock. They come to sit in a warm spot out of the wind. If I could pick my next life, being a big piece of granite in a location like this would be a good choice. I'd have a view and be in the center of things.

This might have been the view George Back saw in 1834. Before the main expedition set out in the spring of 1835, Back and three others traveled by Indian canoe in the fall up the chain of lakes I bypassed, Artillery, Clinton-Colden, and Aylmer, looking for the headwaters of the Thlew-ee-choh, or Great Fish River. Locating the river that fall would save precious time the next spring. His guide was an Indian, Maufelly, who thought he could find the headwaters of this legendary river. None of the other natives claimed to have seen it. In fact, they questioned its existence. Back not only needed it to be there, he needed it to flow north. If they found a river and it flowed east, landing them in Hudson Bay and not on the Arctic coast, his commission to map as much of the Arctic coastline as the season would allow would be unsuccessful.

Maufelly guided them in fits and starts, frustrating Back with his guesswork. It's hard to blame the guide, because he had been to the river only once, to hunt with his father, when he was six years old. By August 28 they had not found the river. Winter was in the air. Back sent the others north by foot. He remained in their makeshift camp. Becoming anxious about his men, he went to search for them. Instead of the men, he found the river:

> I ascended a hill, from the top of which I discerned, to my great delight, a rapid, evidently connected with the stream which flowed through the narrow channel from the lake. With quickened step I proceeded to trace its course, and, in doing so, was further gratified at being obliged to wade through the sedgy waters of springs. Crossing two rivulets, whose lively ripples ran due north into the rapid, the thought occurred to me, that these feeders might be tributaries to the Thlew-ee-choh; and yielding to that pleasing emotion, which discoverers, in the first bound of their transport, may be pardoned for indulging, I threw myself down on the bank, and drank a hearty draught of the limpid water. . . . The men not making their appearance, I raised a dense smoke, by firing the moss, to apprise them of my situation; and returned to the tent, passing, on my way, a white wolf sneaking towards a deer.

I wish for a white wolf sneaking toward a deer, or caribou, on my way back to the tent. As a consolation, I film a few rocks and my footprints—and feel pretty dumb. When I reach camp I realize the camera's eyepiece is missing. All day I haven't felt one thing or another, except pleasure thinking of Captain Back. Now I feel a sinking feeling realizing the eyepiece is lost. Not a large loss, except for what it symbolizes. As I try to retrace my steps, I feel hot prickles up and down my neck. On the esker my footsteps are visible, but finding my tracks on the spongy moss and alder patches is impossible. I crisscross the area until I find the eyepiece lying to the side of my track. Leaning over to pick up that dumb little piece of black rubber, I am as thrilled as if I've found some money on the street at home. It isn't much, but losing it represented carelessness, and carelessness can kill me here.

Far to the north of where I stand, a large bird glides on the wind against a shifting background of dramatic white and deep gray clouds. I watch it tilt sideways and fall off the wind out of sight. I turn to go back, imagining myself walking along the back of a blond whale while it surfaces for a thousand-year moment out of the tundra sea.

George Back and his party began their journey toward the Great Fish River, or Thlew-ee-choh, on June 7, 1834. The three large lakes leading to the lake I'm camped on were thawed only enough to create hard going for his eight men and their two dogs. The dogs needed leather booties tied to their paws for protection from the sharp "candle ice." Over this rotting ice they pulled or carried five thousand pounds of supplies and equipment, including their boat, a thirty-foot rowing craft built on the shore of Artillery Lake earlier that spring.

They had spent a miserable winter in a small cluster of cabins that they built on the shore of Great Slave Lake. Around them camped and hovered many starving Indian families and equally hungry wolves. The wolves caught Back's dog: the dog was rescued, but it did not recover from its broken back. Although Back's party had adequate supplies, and it tormented his conscience to see families of Indians starving, he knew if he gave away more than a small portion of what he had, his own men might not survive. The toughest month was April, but by the end of May, everyone's prospects looked brighter. During those long, dark winter months, Back must have thought of his other two inland Arctic expeditions, each with Sir John Franklin, and how, though he was a Royal Navy man, his career was evolving in the tundra, instead of the ocean.

After the Napoleonic war, the British navy shifted the focus

of its energies to geographical exploration. One aim was to discover a Northwest Passage from the Atlantic to the Pacific Ocean,
across the top of America. For many men, this became a quest.
During the early nineteenth century, several overland expeditions
were undertaken: two of these were led by John Franklin, later
knighted for his efforts. With Franklin on both expeditions was
George Back, whose primary role on the first expedition was as
an artist. Back distinguished himself on both expeditions, but
especially during the first, when he saved Franklin and several
other men from starvation by snowshoeing hundreds of miles for
help. The 1834 expedition to the mouth of the Great Fish River
was Back's first full command.

Not only would his party have to discover their way down
the Great Fish River; in order to return to their safe haven, they
would have to travel back up it before winter. Would he lose
men? Would he be successful in his endeavor to map unknown
shoreline? Whatever doubts gnawed at him in the spring, whatever his thoughts might have been, he was thrilled the day he
departed the dreary winter camp:

> There is something exciting in the first start even upon
> an ordinary journey. The bustle of preparation—the
> act of departing, which seems like a decided step
> taken—the prospect of change, and consequent
> stretching out of the imagination—have at all times the
> effect of stirring the blood, and giving a quicker motion
> to the spirits. It may be conceived then with what
> sensations I set forth on my journey into the arctic
> wilderness.

A copy of his journal will allow me to compare what I see
to his river of 153 years before. A friend photocopied and reduced
Back's journal, making it possible to carry. As opposed to other

early North American wilderness, the Back River should have remained unchanged. I'll see.

I need no passport to get here, yet this is as foreign a place as any in the world—more than most, as it is now devoid of permanent human habitation. People pass through here, or fly over, but only a few live in it without importing everything from the outside world. The several thousand Indian and Inuit former residents who understood the aspects of this land that intrigue me, aspects not mentioned in the reference books, the histories, tourist brochures, and scientific treatises about the tundra, succumbed to outside influence long ago. In the present-day pursuit of naming, knowing, and controlling nature, it's not customary to speak of spirits, or the spirit of the land. The older Inuit and Indians were versed in these dimensions, worlds as alive as any other, but revealed only to them. Like the mysteries of the loon, the tundra remains the land between the facts. To travel safely here you need a shadow passport, and some luck.

Tonight I'll begin to travel. At the conclusion of his journey, Back described the river that lies ahead of me:

> This then may be considered as the mouth of the Thlew-ee-choh, which, after a violent and tortuous course of five hundred and thirty geographical miles, running through an iron-ribbed country without a single tree on the whole line of its banks, expanding into fine large lakes with clear horizons, most embarrassing to the navigator, and broken into falls, cascades, and rapids, to the number of no less than eighty-three in the whole, pours its waters into the Polar Sea.

Over years of canoeing, I've learned to mistrust maps, and my memory, enough not to be lulled by them into a false security, or traumatized by an artificial danger. Maps are useful, but it's the unknown, the unexpected, and what I don't see that gets me in trouble.

Rested and feeling good after the first days, I set out to paddle all night, eager to travel as a nomad, to begin my journey. For the past two days there have been only whispers of cloud at the horizon's rim. There are no mosquitoes or black flies. It's early evening as I start and the light will remain dusklike until morning. Half a mile out of sight of Sussex Lake, the number of rocks sticking up in the river begins to grow. I see room to maneuver, but soon the rocks force me away from shore. Eventually, in the middle of the river, I'm stuck. *Loon* has a rock at her bow and stern. The gentle current holds her pinned. Between the rocks is black, deep water. By standing on rocks I inch forward, nudging and guiding *Loon* through the tight spots. I keep thinking, Only another ten yards and we'll be fine. I'm stuck again. I can't move backward or sideways or closer to shore.

With hands on my hips, I stand on a rock looking at *Loon*. The sun has dipped below the horizon and I sense a rising stillness in the land. Only three things move: myself, the water, and the crescent moon. The sliver ripens in color as the sun disappears, until its comma shape glows in the darkened sky. After every clunk of the paddle, every scrape of the canoe or my boot on a rock, things seem quieter. The noises I make don't carry far. They occur and end the way a knife pierces paper.

I lift each package out of the canoe, place them all on a rock, lift the canoe, and carry it the ten yards to open water. I carry everything over to it and begin again. I get stuck again, and repeat the game. Playing a strange type of hopscotch, I jump from rock to rock. I liked playing hopscotch with my sisters, but this evening I play on unforgiving squares with seventy pounds on my back. A few long portages would make more sense. To portage is to carry the gear around an obstacle. Portaging at the beginning of the summer is painful work; I'm not in shape and everything seems heavy. Seeing more open water ahead, I'm enticed back in to the canoe. I'd like *Loon* to do the work, but in fifteen minutes we're stuck again.

The end of my first night-paddle is a long portage, around the rock-choked headwaters of the river. I am tired but accepting. Even though my muscles are soft and my feet unused to the broken terrain, the consistent relay of first carrying a load, then ambling back for the next, is less annoying than the staccato progress earlier in the evening. On every portage of the summer I'll have four trips to make. I carry the canoe with two paddles; the shafts can slide to the blades, forward and back, lengthening or short-ening the tumpline looped between them, lifting the canoe's weight off my shoulders onto my neck, or vice versa. When I raise *Loon* for our first long walk, I find the tumpline tied too short around the midthwart, pinching my neck. After I retie it, the canoe's weight across my shoulders feels good. To hear the creak of the wood and the rubbing of the paddles, to feel the canoe's balance, makes me bless Denny for building such a fine, light-weight craft. She weighs sixty-two pounds.

Growing up, I was lucky to have woods around me. I was always in them, kicking around, but no one ever mentioned the idea of a shadow passport or a spiritual dimension. Woods were woods. Boston's wilderness was tamed a long time ago.

My friend Nate and I played endless hours of cowboys and Indians. He got to be the Indian because I had the cowboy outfit: chaps, vest, hat, holster, and two white plastic-handled capguns. Lots happens in the woods. Once we came across two unsus-pecting sisters of mine. Nate and I referred to them as the Newts. They were absorbed in creating a miniature village by a small stream. We spied on them while they erected many houses, a bridge across the stream, built roads, granaries, schools—all out of twigs and leaves—a civilization in the wilderness. We watched quietly, waiting for the Newts to finish and leave. They finally went to get my father, to show him the triumph of their labors. Before they returned, Nate and I raided their village: we wrecked everything. Not more than one or two stick-and-leaf houses remained when the Newts returned with my father. That we had knocked everything down wasn't as maddening to them as were my father's complimentary remarks about how nice the nonexistent village looked. When my father left, the hunt began.

My sisters flew after us with a vengeance. Nate acted quickly, escaping to the relative safety of his own house, but there was nowhere for me to hide, except deeper in the woods. At home, I'd be a dead duck. As my sisters were older and bigger, they could pretty well do what they wanted, once they caught me. This terrifying thought helped propel me through the woods, but my cowboy outfit, especially the chaps, was no help. Eventually I tripped and they caught me. One of them held me down, while the other ran home for rope. They tied me, cowboy suit and all, to a tree. They piled dry leaves and sticks around my feet, lots of them. One of my sisters produced two wooden kitchen matches. I'll never forget the rasping sound of a wooden match-head on a sandpaper striker. My eyes were popping out of my head. They each held a lighted match close to my face. Terrified, I stopped screaming long enough to listen to their demands. If I didn't agree and promise to do *everything* they said, they'd burn me up. I agreed. Ever since they've maintained they were kidding. They would never have lighted the pile of sticks, pine needles, and dry leaves around my feet. Never. But what if, just acciden-tally, a match had dropped in the pile? I was pretty well tied to that tree.

Carrying the wannigan, I concentrate on each step, not to slip or to step on a loose rock. I have a bad ankle from playing high school sports. Even when I walk down a flat sidewalk, my ankle can go out. Instead of resisting a fall, I tumble over in a heap. Of all things, breaking a limb, spraining my ankle, or cutting myself badly scares me the most.

The sky seems suspended in twilight. I wait for a deeper progression of night, and realize there isn't going to be any. At home, or in Yellowknife, when I walk into a house for the night, my conversation with the sky ends. To cross a threshold is to enter a human thought. To wake up in a house is to find the next day has begun without me. Here I am working all night under a peculiar sky. There is a certain deepening of twilight, then it holds, goes no farther, for what seems an unusual eternity: Is it the end of the former night? or the beginning of the next day? The light is the same. I finish portaging my last load shortly after the sun rises. Thankfully, I pitch my tent and crumble into sleep.

The next day is the same. I take the hot daytime off, napping and lazing around. In the evening I begin the slow, tedious process of moving through the river's rock fields. The raking light butters every leaf, every grass blade, every rock.

I hear more sounds tonight, especially bird calls, but silence is the loudest sound, if that is possible. The burring call of a ptarmigan at the river's edge heightens the silence of the tundra as it scuttles among the rocks, surfacing once in a while on top of a rock to survey the terrain and chortle its cry. The quack of a red-breasted merganser passing upriver and the underlying hum of how many million tiny insect wings? All these sounds on a windless night, plus my own noises, stir the silence a little and play a halting accompaniment to the land.

As on the first night, I eventually forget the aesthetics. I'm again stuck. I make another long portage. Deep in the twilight, I pass Icy River, named by Captain Back because its ice and snow never completely melt. At the end of a carry the wide bay in front of me reflects the orange sunset. During the night it becomes the blazing orange sunrise. The line of hills across the bay divides the sky from the water, but they could be reversed, water for sky, so perfectly do they mirror one another. For a moment, this dark line of hills seems a black, vast nothingness, a gigantic rent in the seamless fabric of earth and heaven.

⌐ ⌐ ⌐

The wind is blowing today, no clouds, just wind. I'll rest on my seventh day. I think I am through the worst of the river's upper shallows, but I'm not sure. I scout ahead. Half an evening's work and I should reach a narrows that leads to open water and to Muskox Lake.

I find three treasures on my walk: two bones and a thought. The larger bone is a caribou's vertebra. Time and sun and wind have smoothed it, bleached it, made it lightweight. The second bone is smaller, cinnamon-colored and heavy, a bone chip in the shape of a flying goose, although this bone goose has just one wing. I found it lying at the edge of the water, among pebbles. The caribou vertebra will make a pedestal for my miniature bone goose.

The third treasure is the pawprint of a large wolf. Walking back to camp, I imagine why I found it so exciting. Another person might see it as the mark of a predator whose kind is decimating the dwindling caribou herds. To another, it would mean additional income from selling the skin, if he could shoot the wolf. To a scientist studying wolves, the print would mean the chance to study a specimen, maybe attaching a radio tracking device. To still another, the print might evoke an uninformed, primal fear in the pit of his stomach. I did not see the wolf drag down a caribou or pounce on a lemming. I hadn't even seen the wolf. It's enough to know there still are wolves; to know there's a place more theirs than mine; to know neither they nor this wild place have yet been tamed out of existence.

The last several days have been windy, too windy to make paddling worthwhile. I can paddle into a headwind, but conserving my energy makes better sense. The predominant wind is from the north or northeast, the river's direction. I'll have to contend with headwinds all summer, but I hadn't expected to be stopped by one this early. I'm lucky not to be on those large lakes trying to contend with wind as well as ice. Wind can break up rotten ice, by blowing it away, but it can just as easily pin me down by blowing ice into the open leads or on top of me.

It's cloudy. It's late. I finish eating and clean the dinner pot in a small puddle between two rocks. Returning to my tent under a rise, enough of a brow to break the wind, I put my pot down in front of the tent. I turn to go on a walk. On top of the small rise sits a wolf. My quick turn hasn't disturbed him. He remains sitting, regarding me as he would any new curiosity in the neighborhood. He is a white wolf. (I don't know why I think it is a male wolf, but I do.) I waver, but decide we may as well become acquainted. I walk slowly toward him. As I approach he gracefully rises and trots off, disappearing behind the brow of the knoll. As I walk, over the rise, I see him again, watching me. I bow to him and continue walking. Every time I come within forty feet, he trots off. We progress this way across the tundra until he tires of our game. One last time he rises and trots off. He never looks back. My eyes follow him. On the other side of a pond, in the quiet, gray evening light, the wolf changes from a white wolf, into a white shape, to a white spot, then a white speck. He melts into nothing among the ruckus of small and large rocks on the far side of the pond.

JULY 9

It has been eighteen days.

Rain fell last night; continues today. I am in the tent. Two ptarmigan appear at the river's edge. The male is clucking. He hasn't lost his winter feathers, the lower two-thirds of his body remains white. As he walks, each foot is gently raised and set down. With his ruffled leg-coverings he gives the impression of a highly trained dancer in warm-up clothes. Already his mate has her summer camouflage. She blends into the tangle of twigs and old grass among the rocks. She walks quietly, close to the water. Once she raises her left leg to scratch furiously behind her neck. A gull passes overhead. The ptarmigan shrink down defensively, until they realize it is not an owl, a jaeger, or a falcon. Their "burr" erupts into a call somewhere between a motor misfiring and one starting up. As though the two are one body, they lift off in a whir of wings. I poke my head a little further into the rain in time to see them lock in their crescent-shaped wings to glide around a boulder. Four wings stiff as winter, four white feathered fingernail moons gliding through the rain.

The raindrops play tiddlywinks with the loose pieces of moss outside the tent door. In wetness, ground colors deepen. Small raindrops gather on any undersurface, hanging like liquid bats, capable of falling, but not flying. In the slick world of the rocks and pebbles there's always light, even in this rainstorm. Each surface is white with the light's brightest reflection. As I lie watching, I think about how I got here.

There are four ways to fund an expedition: you can write yourself a check, someone else can write you a check, you can work and save, or you can raise the funds. For me, the first two possibilities did not exist, the third would mean I'd be going on the trip in five more years, not this summer. I took a deep breath and began fund-raising in November. I'd need to leave Boston at the end of May, which meant if I didn't have what I needed by the end of March or the middle of April, I wasn't going. I'd need that last month to pack and organize and to test equipment. Transportation in and out of the tundra is the single most expensive item in the budget. I would save money by driving back and forth to Yellowknife. I'd require new equipment as well as a safety net of money in case my plans shifted. Through the film and my writing I wanted to contribute to the effort to help us respect the planet. I wanted to share with others the benefits of solitude and the connectedness to life it offers us. Early on, an old friend, Sam, said, "It's a good idea. Here's a check." Other than that, I was a committee of one prepared every day to hear "No."

Next I needed a sponsoring group, so a donor could see that his or her contribution was tax deductible. Earthwatch in Boston and The Explorers Club in New York backed me. Unfortunately, their sponsorships were not official until the end of January, which trimmed my fund-raising time by two months: now I had from February until April. Before sending a letter to prospective donors, I was actively visiting and discussing my idea with people who knew me. Once past the February starting mark, I returned to show them I hadn't been kidding.

I mailed 300 letters to individuals and received 150 positive responses.

One of my first visits was to an older couple who lived near Boston. I went for lunch. My first mistake was not to have fore-warned them I was fund-raising. I hadn't realized it myself until I was asked what I was up to. Haltingly, I launched into a de-scription of the trip, the rigors of traveling alone, the goals I had for writing about it. The husband, in his seventies, was a man well used to fending off open palms. As soon as he realized where my narrative was leading, he gobbled his dessert. While I talked, an invisible mist settled between us. He began to bang the left side of his head gently with his palm. As I approached that awkward moment of actually asking for money, he began to twiddle with his hearing aid, which responded by making a hor-rible high-pitched whistling noise. He shuffled off toward another room. His wife and I finished our dessert, and to my amazement she pledged a contribution.

Surprisingly, people who hunted, or fished, or canoed, or studied in the Arctic themselves were the least interested in my expedition. One such man invited me to his office.

"What can I do for you, Rob? Oh, yes, your letter. I didn't read it, but tell me a little about what you're up to." I told him.

He was quiet. Then he said, "You know, people like you get my goat. I *work* for my money. I fund-raise for charities I believe in, and you are not one. I see no reason to pay for your summer vacation."

If he'd read my letter we might have had this conversation on the phone, or not at all. "That's okay," I said. "If you don't have the imagination to see any value in my expedition, I wouldn't want to take up more of your time either." It was rude, but he grumbled and wrote out a small check.

Mr. No-imagination raised a good point. What was the validity of my endeavor for other people? The benefits of solitude sounded pretty vague.

Not many perceive the Arctic as relevant, but everyone has gone to a school or college, or has children in one, so many donors accepted my offer to lecture or appear at a school of their choice. The school faculties gladly booked me as an hour's slide lecture or a day's seminar. In one case I taught nature-writing skills for a week to the best and worst English students. They began to see the necessity of preserving wildness and solitude.

I begin my tenth night-paddle, approaching Muskox Lake in extreme quiet. Towering cumulus clouds sit at the edge of the horizon, brought to earth by their reflection in the water. In the half-light of midnight a red-throated loon swims along the edge of an ice floe. It paddles smoothly through the water-clouds, like some outrider from Olympus.

A day's-end hush settles over what has been hectic under the powerful sun. The ice is brittle. The slight tremor of the loon's wake loosens innumerable cylindrical pieces that jangle, like pieces of a crystal chandelier. The loon bows; it pokes its head through the reflected clouds and occasionally disappears, slipping effortlessly into the world on the other side of the sky.

I've never seen a more handsome bird. Its profile is a dark

Z against the water. The gray head and white belly, the dark-red triangle at the throat, the hint of yellow from the top of the head down the back of the neck, the ruby eye.

It swims again along the ice and suddenly leans its neck out and gives a plaintive cry. Unanswered, it throws a lonely, eerie note into the twilight, one I feel echo deep inside me and reverberate long after the loon disappears.

I reach Muskox Lake. In two days I will rendezvous with Chris, Beekman, Denny, and Susanne. One day to paddle the lake and another to reach our meeting place at the foot of the lake. I'm in no hurry. I camp and sleep.

This morning thunderclouds appear; no lightning, just loud cracks. The storm is passing south of me, a big, black spider crawling across the landscape. I've been lax about pegging the tent down, but today I do everything to protect myself from the north and northeast. I picked an embankment to pitch in the lee of, but the storm comes rolling in from the southwest.

The thunderclouds turn the landscape dour. There is power in their varying intensities of piled-up grayness. Rushing ahead of the storm's dark center are white-capped waves. In front of me the retained heat in the stones evaporates the first raindrops. The front growls toward me as I pack up to begin another paddle. I welcome the cool breeze after four hot days.

The rain continues, but I move ahead. I bend and stroke, bend and stroke. My body becomes a human bellows pushing heat out the neck of my raincoat. Around me water reflects sky. Sky bends to touch earth in the water. If the eye is the mirror of the soul, would that make water God's mirror?

I stop for lunch. Drifting on calm, gray water, I eat cheese and nuts. I begin to paddle again. I see a swimming rock ahead. As I approach, the shape moves more quickly to shore, begins to grow larger, and finally appears as a young caribou. Reaching the shallows, its wet gangliness is a caricature of itself. It looks back at me, then ahead into the landscape. The caribou is exhausted, shivering in the water. This calf is on its own, separated from mother and family group. Still quivering, it climbs onto land. After a few tentative steps, it lowers its head in a halfhearted attempt to eat grass. How long will this calf survive before falling prey to a wolf, or the weather? This gray day and uncaring drizzle make me think this caribou's chances aren't good.

I reach the narrows of Muskox Lake and camp on a point facing an island. The head of the rapids is to my left. I'm at the rendezvous. Any number of fish are rising, creating delicate rings in the water or larger swirls. Less often, one of them leaps, landing back in the water with a solid *thwack*. Across the narrows is a high hill I'd like to investigate tomorrow.

I missed the Fourth of July, so five days after the fact I walk to the promontory across the river to celebrate. The sun has returned. I follow a streambed where the right amount of moisture and wind protection allow the alders in the gully to grow shoulder high. Usually tundra alders scrape along between the rocks, fanning out near the ground, hardly reaching knee height. Their small, dead twigs provide the only available firewood. Because they retain little water, even green alder branches burn in a hot fire. Collecting enough dead twigs to cook over is tedious work, especially near the Arctic coast where wood is scarce. I enjoy gathering an armful for a small friendship fire, but mostly I depend on the Mountain Systems Research (MSR) stove and a gallon of fuel for cooking. If I bake this summer, it will be in the pressure cooker. Other than that, it's frying-pan bannock or deep-fried doughnuts, or as Horace Kephart called them, "quoits."

Kephart was an interesting woodsman. His book, *Camping and Woodcraft*, first published in 1906, is a classic. He conveys wisdom through anecdotes, as when he describes the difference between an Indian walking through the forest and a white man. The white man, used to flat city streets, is always off balance. An Indian could be turned to bronze at any time and his statue would never fall over. Thinking of this helps me place my feet. The wilderness Kephart described in the United States is gone, as are the frontier people, Indians, and wilderness travelers he vividly portrayed. What remains wild in North America is relegated to pockets, small islands, the edges of which are constantly nibbled at by pressure from the human world. The rest of the wilderness is caught between a rock and a hard place. When it is turned into parks, preserves, or sanctuaries, large sums of money are spent, boundaries set, public interest stimulated. Everything outside the park boundaries becomes fair game for exploitation, and inside comfort is increased to attract people. Finland is the only country to divide its national parkland into thirds: one zone for the tourists, one wilderness zone for more hardy campers, and one larger "natural" zone sealed off and retained in its original state.

The streambed leads me to the promontory from the south side. It's hot. It takes me an hour to get there. As I clamber up the scree to the promontory's base, ten ptarmigan erupt from the rocks. They scatter like a starburst of fireworks. The suddenness of our encounter makes my heart race. I am intensely grateful that they were not bears. I see the scooped-out holes they made in the warm dirt. They convene here for conversation and a good dust bath.

Standing on top, I look out over backcountry I will never visit. I see my first glimpse of the Heywood Mountains, a thin blue stripe to the north. I stand looking down at the tear of mountains in the distance, and the sparkling surface of several ponds, the closest reflecting the vibrant blue sky. The tangled browns and coming greens of new vegetation blend with the dense alder cover in the gully, a green mat of pubic hair hiding the secret of the stream I followed. My eyes feel the solidness of the tips of toffee-brown and gray rocks that punctuate the land. I detect no animal life, but feel many small and large eyes are carefully monitoring me.

At the edge of the alders, I see what I take to be a pair of swans on their way to a pond. I barely discern their bobbing necks against the leaves and alder branches blowing in the breeze. Perhaps they don't see me. I leave the raised ground and move to intercept them. I try to stay low to the ground, bent forward in a duck walk. I am unable to see if they lead or I follow. When I arrive at the pond, no swans. I wait. Half an hour passes, still nothing. Their plans must have changed. On the way back, as I amble to the shore and *Loon*, I come across my "swans": a large rack of caribou antlers, bleached white and sticking up.

The day ends with a small feast. To celebrate my independence, I drink a healthy ration of overproof Lamb's Navy Rum. They say a little goes a long way. I have more than a little. Only after drinking my ration do I have the courage to film. I take the movie camera up on a rise. Forgetting that I have the microphone cable plugged into it and the mike hooked onto me, I walk back down the slope. The microphone cable becomes taut. The camera begins to follow me, then falls facefirst in the dirt. The plug into the camera shears off and the camera's lens is badly scratched. Having ruined one camera, I decide, Why stop here? I bring out one of the remaining two, the Elmo. I film a segment I call "Tundra Waterbeds," featuring the squishy ground under the tent. I don't exactly remember what I say because shortly afterward I collapse on my tundra waterbed, drunk. This is not smart. The weather could shift, or a temperance bear might appear in camp looking for sinners.

Like magic, one moment nobody's here; the next minute— *poof!*—the film crew arrives. Is this what happens when you die? Meeting your friends again, either in heaven or hell, full of questions: How's it been? What's happened? How's my dad?

Beekman tells me my father is the same. They have not

determined why his blood won't clot. He's had numerous transfusions. He is lucky he is still alive.

After the pilot refuels, he flies ahead several hundred miles along the river with Chris and Beekman to drop off a cache of food I'll pick up near the end of the trip, after the big lakes. Carrying camera equipment has displaced food supplies that I'll replenish from this cache. Chris wants to put more film and a spare camera ahead of me. Denny puts in an extra paddle. Everything, except the paddle, fits in the same size wannigan as I carry. That cache is something to look forward to reaching in a month.

The rest of us fix camp. Watching Denny and Susanne cope with the bugs makes me realize I am used to them. Quite a few mosquitoes are out. Listening to the crew's remarks, I relive my first days here, feel again the light, the space, the colors of the lichen, the land's flatness. Although to them it seems quiet, their presence is more noise than I have heard since Larry's plane flew away. I love it.

Once more the loudness of a plane shatters the stillness. Beekman and Chris are back. The plane drops them off and leaves. It will return for them in four days.

Beekman takes over the kitchen. Chris and Susanne fuss with their camera equipment. Denny and I look at *Loon*. The next days are a mixture of hard work and agreeable companionship. Denny's presence means a lot to me. Better than anyone, he lays to rest the jitters I have about what lies ahead. He makes light of them, reminding me to just keep breathing. The rest will take care of itself.

Not only did he build *Loon*, he built my first solo canoe, *Monkey*, in 1979. Before that, we went on our first long canoe trip down the Eastmain River in Quebec. Since then our lives have often crisscrossed, if not headed the same way, at least following the same scent.

When Denny built *Monkey* he had a shop and an assistant. He thought he could earn a living building canoes. He had the customers, but the workmanship and hours required to build a good canoe cut severely into the profit. He began doing other things. I wasn't sure he'd build me another canoe. After a long mull he said, "Rob, certain people like to sharpen things, pack things, and tie things up. You're one of those. So am I. I'll build you your canoe." His logic wasn't clear to me, but that's often the way with Denny. What he has really built me is a clear-sighted philosophy.

Denny built my canoe in his living room in Stockbridge, Massachusetts. I helped him move in two wood stoves, more, he said, to show me his good intentions than to spend the winter there. We covered the floor with plastic, taped it down, and laid a dropcloth over it.

The house Denny and his family live in, built in the 1890s by an English professor from Yale University, is the house Denny grew up in. It commands a view of Monument Mountain. The wood paneling around the living room where *Loon* was born has an inscription carved under the ceiling in twelve-inch letters:

> *And this our life, exempt from public haunt,*
> *Finds tongues in trees, books in the running brooks,*
> *Sermons in stones, and good in everything.*

The quote comes from *As You Like It*. What the professor left out is as telling as what he had carved. The preceding lines in the play are:

> *Sweet are the uses of adversity,*
> *Which, like the toad, ugly and venomous,*
> *Wears yet a precious jewel in his head.*

In our own way, we took these lines to heart. To Denny it said, if you can embrace what you fear, if you can kiss the toad, then what you fear may turn into its opposite. I had recently spent two years in New York City, two very toadlike years. I did not feel inclined to kiss them then, or today.

Loon is a strip-built canoe with a fiberglass skin and a wood core. Denny used Sitka spruce on the bottom, western red cedar up the sides. The spruce is tougher than the cedar, but the cedar is lighter than the spruce. Mixing the two allowed Denny to save weight and gain strength where it was needed. He built up each end where he knew the most abuse would occur; otherwise she would have weighed less than her sixty-two pounds.

He chose "S" glass to cover the wood rather than Kevlar or fiberglass because of its ability to bond more completely with the wood once the resin is applied. The fibers in "S" glass run one way as opposed to the two-way weave of traditional fiberglass. Optimal strength is achieved by laying one skin on bow to stern and a second skin on perpendicular to the first. On the inside of the canoe, Denny laid a skin side to side to act as one rib throughout. He built in two flotation chambers, one at each end, from pieces of tough, flexible mahogany plywood. Inside the stern chamber he glued a small survival package containing a lighter, some fishhooks and lures, fishing line, a piece of mirror: "Just an added incentive for you to stay with the canoe, if you happen to tip over," he said.

Denny procrastinated and diddled. We both knew he wouldn't have the canoe ready until the June day I left. In May I went with Chris Knight to film Denny at work.

Denny was getting ready to put the gunwales on. We helped him carry the canoe outdoors, set it on two sawhorses, and secure it with wooden wedges. *Loon*'s most unusual feature is its tumblehome, the sharp curve of its sides in toward the canoe's centerline. This gives *Loon* a racy aspect. Stability isn't sacrificed; in fact, it increases: it helps diminish the impact of oncoming waves and provides an added buoyancy as the bow sinks deeper in the water.

"That is," Denny said, "until the water's over the gunwales."

We thought hard about a spray skirt. I've never liked a full spray skirt, because often in a rapid I need to stand up to get a better look at the water ahead. Statistically, more drowning deaths occur with fully skirted canoes, perhaps because the full spray skirt provides a false sense of security for paddlers who then take on bigger white water than they should.

Besides shedding rain, I need the skirt only to throw off the occasional wave. "In that case," Denny said, "let's use the lightest material. Now, what about snaps?" I hate snaps. Especially on cold, wet days, it's painful to fasten or unfasten tightly fitted snaps. So Denny designed an ultra-lightweight spray skirt, fastened to the canoe with Velcro. He glued and stapled a two-inch strip of Velcro to the canoe and sewed a thinner strip to the edge of the spray skirt. I wouldn't need to be finicky about putting it on. I just position the skirt and run my hands over it to seal it below the gunwales. The larger Velcro strip catches the smaller one. Conversely a flick of the wrist and off it comes. The skirt's simplicity won't tempt me to leave it off.

Attaching gunwales is a tricky part of canoe building. It takes more than one set of hands, a lot of clamps, and fast, sure movements. The quickness required is related to the time available after mixing the resin. Prior to mixing our batch of resin, we laid out the two gunwales, the necessary tools, all Denny's clamps, and a few he had borrowed.

Denny hesitated. Finally he told me we didn't have enough clamps. He said he knew where he'd find some. As he left, he muttered how handy another person would be to hold the gunwales in place. In my eagerness to help, I thought of John, a woodworker Denny had taken me to see the day before. We had borrowed all his available clamps.

I drove the short distance to John's house and found him in his shop. Along the walls hung woodworking tools of different types, sizes, and uses. To me it looked like a medieval torture chamber.

John's various projects were in different stages of completion. There were thin slices of wood stacked on top of each other under immense pressure in a large vise. Long wooden slats were being coaxed into a curved shape by another machine. Around every saw lay cut-out chunks, strips, and limbs of different types of wood. Piles of sawdust clung to the sides of the machines that did the cutting like potting soil for these wood-eating plants.

We chatted. I told John we were going to put the gunwales on the canoe. Could he possibly come and help? Denny hadn't sent me. This was my idea. I'd like to see my canoe get finished. I'd even pay him. He thought about it, but not for long.

"I like Denny," he said. "I like him using my tools too, because he returns them the way I gave them to him. But to work with him would make me nervous. The other day at his house, I saw him using a wood chisel as a splitting wedge. Everything he makes turns out to be beautiful, especially that canoe, but he's unorthodox. It would make me anxious just to watch him."

Looking at his orderly workshop, I could see what he meant. At Denny's everything had its place too. It's just that only he, or his son, Ben, knew where that place was. Tools lost their names once they entered Denny's house. Ben's and Denny's projects were made out of mixtures of "whatsits" and "thats," put together by a process that would have pleased Dr. Seuss.

Later that afternoon, with the gunwales clamped in place, I followed Denny as he searched for something to clamp two big pieces of wood together. We walked halfway around his house carrying the just-glued pieces of wood, until Denny spied several discarded stone steps.

"Here, pick that end up. Straighten that out. Place the whatsits there."

And sure enough, the pieces of glued wood looking for a squeeze got one between two steps weighing several hundred pounds apiece. I smiled and wondered how nervous this would have made John.

◻ ◻ ◻

The working days with the film crew are hectic, full of small and large excursions. Chris wants to film aspects of the trip I couldn't film myself. The morning of the second day, a bear appears across the river. I see it as I get out of the tent and call to the others. Beekman is already up. Denny and I join him to watch the large taffy-colored grizzly lumber over the uneven tundra. Chris and Susanne are stuck in their tents putting film in their cameras. The bear stops. It notices us. It pushes its snout out in our direction and squints. It walks on. Everyone feels comfortable, until the bear jumps in the water two hundred yards downriver and begins to swim to our side. The nearest tree is three hundred miles south. As a substitute, I offer to let Beekman climb on my shoulders.

Chris appears, camera ready, and says, "Let's go find the bear." Beekman and I opt to stay behind to guard the bacon. They never see the bear, but Denny returns excited because he has answered a question raised the evening before.

Beek had read us a journal entry from the diary of Warburton Pike, an Englishman who had been to Muskox Lake in the 1890s. Pike had come north on a hunting expedition. He described a traditional caribou fording place at the foot of the lake near the rapids where the Inuit hunted. Denny said the bear had used it, and in fact he found the tracks in a gully. The tracks led up from the water. The slope of the gully was as gentle as an airport walkway. On top of a rise there was a pile of rocks: an old hunting blind described in Pike's journal, one rock or a semicircle of rocks an Inuit hunter would hide behind when hunting caribou.

An unexpected arrival, along with the good weather, is the growing number of insects. By the third day there has been a population explosion among the mosquitoes. The black flies are not present in any great number. That pleasure lies north of me, downstream.

On our last night together, the full moon rises. Its splendor catches us off guard. The last rays of the sun are still visible while the first fingernail of lunar color arches over the edge of the eastern landscape. As the small filament begins to grow, astonishment holds us immobile. The roundness threatens to swallow that whole portion of sky. All the while, the sun remains visible at our backs. Chris snaps into action. He tells me to run toward the moon for some pictures. I do, and I don't stop. Long after the moon has lifted off the earth, and they have stopped taking pictures, I continue walking toward its huge saucer shape. There is no delicacy in it. It is powerful and absorbing.

No wonder the Inuit revered the moon. For its blessing, hopeful mothers exposed their genitals to its light. The Caribou Inuit believed that when a person died his spirit flew up to the moon. When you couldn't see the moon, they said she was down on earth distributing spirits into new forms: a rock, a caribou, a fish, a fox, even human beings. All spirit, or *inua*, comes from the moon.

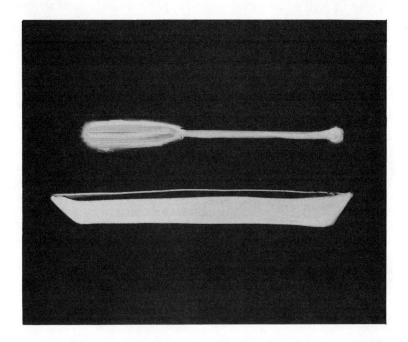

Direct sunlight had left the land, but its glow and the moon's pale light mingled together. I could feel them around me like a cloak. To stand in a place on this earth and see the full moon and feel the sun on my back is to be at the moment's fulcrum. At the water my amble stops. The moon's reflection over the water extends to my feet. I want to reach for it but remember the poet Li Po. Not wishing to emulate his death, I turn back toward camp. Li Po, they say, fell from a boat and drowned as he reached for the moon's watery reflection.

I see a human silhouette jutting above the dark horizon, standing on a large rock. I wonder who it is. I can't help seeing it as myself.

On the last afternoon, I can't prevent myself from missing my friends even before they leave. I have fifty days ahead, the river's whole length. Anything can happen. We take down the tents, careful to pick up any stray pieces of paper and plastic. Late in the day the plane comes. Before they jump from a rock onto the plane's pontoon, I receive and give a hug to each. Denny smiles and says, "Just keep breathing." I stand on the rock watching the plane drift back onto Muskox Lake. It turns and taxis down the lake for takeoff. The plane roars over the water, passing low over my head. I barely raise my arm to wave good-bye. Tears stream down my face. I stand there until nothing is left to see or hear.

Loon is already a mile downstream along with my gear. I pick up a small bag of leftover groceries, a few potatoes, a lemon, some cabbage, and walk slowly to join her.

That night, in a flush of mixed feelings, I skim across the top of sleep. I start dreaming of my dad, then skip to these last four days. In my dream the bear runs the camera. We are no larger than rabbits hopping in front of it. I lie half awake. Unexpectedly a piece of memory successfully avoided for a year surfaces. As if I've opened the window of an Advent calendar, there it is.

I never expected to see Una again, but a year ago in New York at Christmastime in Pennsylvania Station, I did. As far as I knew, she lived in Ireland. That was where she had returned, but now I saw her thirty yards away.

I'd been waiting for a train back to Boston that was delayed by heavy snow. Getting bored, I tried to guess the occupation of each passing stranger: there's a stock broker, a professor, and a bald soprano. Then I saw Una. She could tell, in that odd way one can, someone was watching. She stopped and looked. I waved. She saw me. The station transformed itself into a lopsided purgatory. It wasn't trains people waited for, but other people. We were all there to set each other free, or to set another into motion, arriving from a somewhere headed to a somewhere else.

She wore a red beret that boldly set off the short torrent of her silver-gilt curls. Her slight build and quiet masked a strong spirit. A high forehead and the widow's peak curving into it, along with her prominent cheekbones, heightened her Celtic looks. Several men looked up as she passed. I could feel every

nerve wake up as we said hello. Outwardly calm, too calm, we chatted for several minutes. I no more would have asked her what brought her back to New York than I would have asked her for the moon. A year before she had left our Brooklyn apartment, flown home to Ireland "to pick up a few things," and never come back.

An elderly woman asked us where she could get a newspaper. It took a minute for me to focus, but not Una. Without hesitating, she said, "Behind this wall, around to the left." After the lady walked away, Una met my questioning gaze, saying, "I have no idea, really, but it should be over that way." Same old Una. I was glad when my train was announced. Joining the line of people heading to the train, I turned to smile another good-bye, but she had dissolved back into the crowd she had come out of.

Giving up on the magazine I'd bought for the ride, I thought about Una, the evolution of our love and its ending. We had met on the water. Perhaps that accounted for the indefiniteness I always felt between us. There was much I never understood, except at the end, the hurt.

On the train I fell into restless sleep. I dreamed of Una. It was afternoon light, a winter day. I have no idea whether she could skate, but she was skating. I could see her breath. The sunlight was weak. Clouds passed over the small, tree-lined pond as she skated. No one else was present. The ice was new, black ice. A shiver raced through it when she pushed onto the ice. She had on high black figure skates and a dark-blue skater's skirt, while her legs showed white in between. She wore red mittens and earmuffs. She practiced turns and different moves, slowly, deliberately, enjoying her animal strength. Other times she just skated. The skates made satisfying sounds as the blades scraped and cut into the ice. A fine white tracery evolved on the surface, fine white lines left behind by her skate blades, crisscrossing each other, some made patterns, others chaos, but each one left a white cut in the ice.

The sun began to set. In the dream I no longer watched—I was the ice. Each push of Una's blades ran across me, cut me. Each fine white tracery was a slice across my chest, or my wrists, or my stomach. Each maneuver she made, I felt pain, but admiration too. The sun appeared red for one last moment, skewered on the dark jagged tree line around the pond, its light staining the ice an even deeper, blood red. Una continued to skate. A light snow began to fall. She went into a spin that became closed. At that moment her body became an indistinct blur, the point of her right skate boring deep into my heart.

Waking up, I found myself still on the train, headed to Boston. I shook, the way a dog shakes climbing out of water. Our relationship lasted three years. It began with sporadic visits, countless letters, and numerous expensive trans-Atlantic phone calls. Then I found I had to visit England. As England was next door to Ireland, I could visit Una for Christmas. That suited her, as she wanted me to see her home, meet her mother, and stay awhile. I knew Una was close to her mother, but not until I arrived did I appreciate how close. Una met me at the airport. We kissed lightly, and drove through a tangle of roads and high hedges, very fast and just for fun.

Amid tinkling crystal and the subdued knock of silver knives and forks, I gained my first impressions of the woman I hoped would become my mother-in-law. Her name was Emer. She sat opposite me, next to Lord D., our host. I had arrived only several hours before, and instead of a quiet evening at home, I was spirited off to this sumptuous meal. "Don't worry," said Una. "Everything will be fine." I'm sure it was for her; she sat at the farthest end of the table. I was having a miserable time listening to Emer and Lord D. discuss their friends.

Lord D. asked me what type of stories we told in America. I said, "Where I come from, Maine stories." He asked me to tell them one. I wished I were someone else. I began a story about a young honeymoon couple and the girl's mother. After the marriage, all three—young husband, bride, and her mother—go to Maine for the honeymoon. On the dock in Maine, the mother appears as she is, a substantial piece of work. She wears a sky-blue dress with a wide-brimmed hat to match. She couldn't have weighed under 250 pounds. The young groom's friend is set to run the party over to Swan's Island where they would stay for a week. The tide is out and the mother-in-law can't climb down the ladder to the dock. They have to rig a hoist, lowering her directly into the friend's lobster boat. Out to sea, it's rough and getting worse. The boat begins to pitch and roll. The young man's friend sees that the mother-in-law doesn't take to it. She's at the rail, heaving over the side. That much weight on the side, in a rough sea, is awkward for steering. All of a sudden, the boat levels. The mother's gone overboard. Searching, all they can find is that sky-blue, wide-brimmed hat floating over a mess of bubbles. The bride is distraught and the couple goes home early. As they leave, the young man asks his friend to let him know if anyone should find his mother-in-law.

The proper telling of this story takes a full twenty minutes. I tried to rush the delivery, which I shouldn't have, for the story's sake. For my sake, I should never have started. The end is that after two weeks, the young groom gets a call from his friend, who says they've found her. "She wasn't much to look at when they drug her up. But, funniest thing, she had about fifty of the finest pound-and-a-half lobsters you'd ever wish to see clinging to every part of her." The friend says he put the lobsters in his lobster pound and he wonders where the groom wants him to send the body. There's a pause, then the young man offers this suggestion: "Tell you what. You keep half the lobsters, send me the other half, and set her out again."

Lord D. thought that was pretty good. He laughed, said it was very Roald Dahl, until he saw Emer, who wasn't smiling. The conversation drifted to other things. By the time Lord D. spoke to me again, his reserved manner told me that he had gotten the word about my visit. I knew what Emer had told Una: a few simple reasons why she didn't think I was the man for her daughter.

I was an American.

I wasn't rich.

I lived in an apartment, not a house.

A nature writer had no future.

I must be after their money.

Swaying Emer would be an uphill climb, but I was in love and ready to move mountains. As long as Una stood beside me, I was sure I could.

Lord D. asked me how long my stay would be. I replied I was stopping over for a brief visit with Una and Emer on my way home from England.

"Oh?" he said.

"Yes," I said. "I had the privilege of spending two weeks with one of England's greatest living poets."

"Who is that?" asked Lord D.

"Basil Bunting," I said. He repeated the name to himself and laughed out loud.

"Bunting. Basil Bunting. Sounds more like a bird, or an herb. Emer, have you ever heard of Basil Bunting, famous British poet?"

"Certainly not," replied Emer.

"There, you see," he said, "if we haven't heard of him, he couldn't be very famous."

The main course arrived, pheasant in Cumberland sauce. Most of the people at the table, I discovered later from Una, were Lord D.'s paying guests. He rented his wood during the winter season to wealthy people who wanted to impress their friends and shoot pheasant twice a day. He provided the wood, the pheasant, the gameskeeper, and an occasional meal like this, for which they paid him handsomely.

As I ate my pheasant and studied the happy, healthy-looking crowd, I thought of Basil Bunting living out the remainder of his

days in a small carriage house in Northumberland outside Hex-
ham. He was eighty-five and living two years longer, he said,
than he should have a right to.

I had written Mr. Bunting asking to come for a visit. He
had written back saying come ahead. I had explained that, as an
artist and nature writer, I enjoyed illustrating the work of poets
who love nature. I had then completed two prints: one with the
American poet James Merrill, and one with the Irishman Seamus
Heaney. I hoped one with Basil Bunting would soon join them.

A younger poet, Colin, lived next door, assisting Basil with
what he could no longer do for himself. They were extremely
quiet while I stored my few things upstairs. Everything in the
cottage was simple: wooden tables and chairs, except for one
armchair near the fire with wads of stuffing showing. There was
an alcove in front of a small kitchen that held a dining-room table
and four chairs. In the kitchen was a gas cooker, the kind with
the broiler suspended over the burners. The two rugs were thread-
bare. The fireplace was large and welcoming and burned a mixture
of peat and coal. On the walls around the sitting room were his
books. He had sold most of them, except those inscribed by his
friends: Laura Riding, T. S. Eliot, Ezra Pound, William Carlos
Williams, Louis McNeice, W. B. Yeats, Ford Madox Ford, Ernest
Hemingway, Dylan Thomas, Hugh MacDiarmid, Myrna Loy,
James Joyce, and others whose names I did not recognize.

While I was looking around, Colin and Basil sat at the dining-
room table as if they were my jury. I joined them and we entered
into casual conversation. Out of consideration for Mr. Bunting's
interests, I tried to keep the conversation on literature. This is
what they seemed to want too. I don't know the appropriate
scuttlebutt. They exchanged skeptical glances.

Finally Mr. Bunting sighed and said, "Mr. Perkins, your
knowledge of the literary past is shameful, especially as you call
yourself a literary historian. See"—he turned to Colin—"what
American universities turn out and call scholars!" He was clearly

upset. I was too. His stern gaze turned to confusion when I said I wasn't a literary historian.

"I love animals, the land, and water. I try to write about them and paint them, the best I can."

"You what?" said Mr. Bunting, not believing his ears. They both were quiet. Mr. Bunting looked at Colin, and said, slowly, in his rich Northumberland accent, "Colin, I think this calls for a drink. Let's see how Mr. Perkins likes his drink. Do you drink, Mr. Perkins?"

"I do," I said, solidly as I could.

Colin opened a cupboard in the dining room stuffed with green bottles with the stag's head trademark. Mr. Bunting nodded at them, remarking, "Every goddamn literary hound who comes snooping around me for one more morsel about Paris in the twenties, or my work with Ezra, brings me a bottle of Glenfiddich. That's all they're good for."

We drank a good deal before Basil remembered to start dinner. This consisted of opening a large can of beans and broiling us two sausages apiece. He shuffled back to the table to resume drinking. By now two of the green bottles stood empty on the table. I was fully baked; to my hosts the thought of diluting good scotch was tantamount to being a literary historian. We drank it by the tumblerful, neat.

Soon we smelled smoke, lots of smoke, and saw it rising around the broiler. With a quick shuffle-hop, Basil reached the stove; he yanked the broiler pan and launched the sausages toward the window to his right. They skidded over the floor and tumbled into a greasy heap at the wall. "No harm done," Basil remarked as he scooped them up and put them on our plates.

We continued drinking, and ate the errant sausages. After this initiation, I stayed as a welcome guest and diversion for ten days. The simplicity of Basil Bunting's life was a lesson. A trip into any of the local pubs was an endless stream of observations and pints of lager. Even his car was simply different. It was from the Netherlands. It was driven by two large, thick rubber bands, connecting the engine to the back axle. One afternoon as we crossed a moor, one of the large rubber bands snapped. The car coasted to a stop. While Colin walked for help, Basil and I stood on the road in a tundralike landscape. Clouds blew over the sun, making the scene contract and expand as if we stood in the center of the sensitive pupil of a cosmic eye. The moor's attire was late autumn, a blend of muted browns and yellows. As I stood enjoying the surface play of light and dark, colors and textures, Basil began to talk. He related the history of the place, from the Roman coal mine, just over the rise, to the equally ancient road that led to Hadrian's Wall at the head of the valley. He knew the relation-ships of the different pre-Christian tribes who loved and warred across this moor, how the first Christians were killed and by whom. I felt I listened not to Basil Bunting, but to history itself. Across the moor glided a falcon, hunting. Quietly, Basil watched it rise and fall like a breath. He spoke:

> Have you seen a falcon stoop
> accurate, unforeseen
> and absolute, between
> wind-ripples over harvest? Dread
> of what's to be, is and has been—
> Were we not better dead?
> His wings churn air
> to flight.
> Feathers alight
> with sun, he rises where
> dazzle rebuts our stare,
> wonder our fright.

When we saw Colin returning, he stopped. We fixed the car and drove home. The landscape is a present tense. The history I heard is past, all but forgotten except by people like Basil

Bunting, and they are passing too. The beauty is in the timeless words. The man I met was old. He barely resembled the Mandarin qualities of his young photographs. For a word dreamer like myself, standing by him, watching the hawk, hearing him speak . . .

"What? Oh, I'm sorry. Excuse me. Certainly." At Lord D.'s table the entree had come and gone. Salad and dessert too. Cheese and port were being passed. I had missed it all, caught up as I was in my Northumberland reverie. I went home with Emer and Una that evening full, but not from the meal.

Standing next to the Back River, light-years from that time, I feel oddly transfixed by the mingling of the water's sound with my thoughts. Basil has died, but remembering his hawk reminds me of the raptor I saw riding the wind from the esker.

During the several weeks of my stay, Emer found many ways to let me know I was not going to marry her daughter. My Maine story had drawn a battle line.

At the foot of the field behind their house, a gnarled oak had blown down the previous fall. Five feet thick in places, it lay, with its hundreds of years of knowledge, flat along the ground. Cutting it into firewood became my project. "A good place for him too," Emer remarked to her daughter. "Outside." I made better progress with the tree than with Emer.

A wise man might have seen the entanglement between mother and daughter and stepped aside. Had I been as wise as the oak I was cutting up, I'd have known this.

Emer's small property bordered Lord D.'s larger estate abutted by a stand of oaks. After working on the fallen oak, I'd step into this wood to feel surrounded by the trees' solidness. Sometimes Una would join me. More often I entered alone.

During these winter months, the woods were not silent. Twice a day the pheasant hunters were shooting. I cringed at the heavy salvos of gunfire aimed at those handsome birds.

The pheasants were Lord D.'s cash crop, raised in pens, then set loose to feed in specific areas of the wood. The gamekeeper protected them from all predators—the fox, the mink, the weasel, even neighborhood dogs—except the paying ones. On my walks, I'd find the traps and destroy them, spring them, or set the terrified creatures free. The majority were ingeniously devised and cleverly hidden choke-hold traps. Placed in the animal's path, the trap's thin noose wire tightens on the animal's neck as it runs headfirst into it. The harder the terrified animal struggles, the tighter the noose becomes, the sooner the animal strangles itself. I could tell how well the gamekeeper was doing because each week the birds and animals, either trapped or shot, wound up hung on the fence surrounding the wood. I was pleased to see a decline in the number of bodies after I started taking my walks.

Occasionally cripples or terrified pheasant escapees would whir onto Emer's property. That was fine with her; she liked the thought of having a meal at her neighbor's expense.

Christmas day I rose early. While the rest of the house slept, I slipped the latch on the front door. Overnight the temperature had dropped. Outside my breath became instantly white. The driveway gravel crunched under my feet. I heard a rook's guttural caw; it seemed less the warning it had first sounded to me, and more a laugh. I intended to see the sun rise and to walk in Lord D.'s woods, but I went no farther than Emer's back pasture. There had been a hoar frost: everything was white. Later the sun's warmth would unlock every prisoner, but for now each blade of grass, the trees and even the fallen oak, were transformed by the frost. Nothing moved.

I saw a hare hop into view at the field's edge, stopping by the oak before disappearing through the frozen grass. As I walked, grass blades crackled as if I were breaking glass. I touched a

Queen Anne's lace. It shattered. I went to visit the small brook with which I had discussed Una's and my situation during breaks from splitting rounds of the old oak. The brook was held captive under a thin coat of ice, but its joyful chatter could still be heard. I could see the small waves and air pockets as they lapped at the underside of the ice. Inside the house the two women slept. A shiver ran through me: This is the world of Emer's dreams—beautiful, immobile, firmly controlled. I brushed the thought away and walked back inside to brew some tea.

Some of Emer's objections I could never overcome, but getting a good paying job and eventually owning a house and land were possible. What I didn't take into account was that Emer was capable of producing an infinite number of hurdles. Una suggested we have a trial period together. She would come to America for a visit. We'd decide where to go from there.

Emer collected Georgian silver. She kept her collection in cupboards at the back of the kitchen. She showed it to me one afternoon. I could see how much she knew about the styles and marks and various unique qualities of each piece. Una said it was a good sign that her mother had shown her silver collection to me. That night I woke with a jolt. In my dream, Emer had been showing the collection to me, purring over it. She reached for the last cloth bag, one larger than all the rest, and said, "This is my favorite: my daughter."

The evening was warm the night I left. I could smell spring welling up in the earth, in the grass, in the trees. From a majestic tree the oak was now transformed into firewood. I was bringing a large chip of it home in my pocket, but little of its hundreds of years of understanding had passed into me. It all would, as they say, go up in smoke. But Una was coming to America. That was all I cared about.

Taking advantage of the warm weather, Emer was on all fours working in her garden when I came to say good-bye. I was triumphant knowing Una had decided to follow me in the spring.

Emer was digging up roots. She detested them. She felt they were strangling her garden and would soon head toward her house. If she didn't dig them up, they would take over her world. As she worked, a piece of her usually well-kept hair fell out of place. She pushed it up with the back of her wrist as I approached. I knew she was glad to see me go. In that evening twilight, as we exchanged pleasantries and I turned to leave, it was hard to tell if she included me in her last muttered remark: "It takes so long, so long."

I had a premonition, just then. Una was tangled up with a selfish woman who had a hundred different ways of directing everyone's attention to her. That night, as Una and I kissed good-bye at the airport, we wished a lot from the future. What we wanted, not anything or anyone, not knocking on wood, even on the oak chip in my pocket, could ever bring us.

In the morning beside the river below Muskox Lake, I don't know what to think. To get beyond that relationship I had buried it. Deep. What pried it loose? The jolt of being alone? The tundra?

I brew coffee and cut up a leftover potato for homefries. From my tent, at the head of the second half of Muskox Rapids, I see each side of the river covered in snow. To scout the rapid, I can walk to the end over the snowfield—which may not hold my weight—or I can paddle through the rapid. I opt for careful paddling.

The river dips and twists twice as it winds out of view. My optimism leads me to believe that these two blind sections of river will be the same as the river I can see from where I stand. What I can't see is that the snowfields become the walls of an icy canyon—one I couldn't get out of if I tried. Entering the first canyon, I think how beautifully the sunlight turns the ice blue, how cool the ice makes the air.

Everything seems serene, hardly dangerous.

After committing myself, I perceive the risk. In places the ice walls pinch inward, creating a *whoosh* of strong current. The water's force has eaten away a main channel through the ice and undercut the walls. Small waterfalls, the runoff of melting snow, gush from the top, creating fissures and giant cracks in the wall. Around me large chunks fall into the river. How could I have been this stupid? The next blind curve could be an ice tunnel with no headroom. The current accelerates. I cannot back up. Neither can I climb out over the walls. The image of my dead body, a rag doll smacked up against the ice, makes my stomach contract.

I try to slow down. Occasionally I rest in an eddy behind a rock. At times, skimming along one side, having to bang rocks I can't avoid, I back-paddle furiously. Finally, as if the river yawned, the ice walls step back, the river widens. I float in calm water.

As I drift in safety, I see the image of a painting I saw as a child. It scared me then and it scares me today. An early American painting in the Museum of Fine Arts in Boston shows a naked man in the water with a whaling boat full of men trying to save him. His body glows ghostly white against the dark-green water. His arms stretch out toward the boat. The one thing at ease in the picture is the shark. Its enormous jaws are poised to bite. After I saw the painting, my small arm never strayed over the edge of the bed without my conjuring visions of that shark.

I spend the night on a rock outcrop farther down the rapids, but not out of them. Before stopping, I pass the first large tributary feeding the Back: the Contwoyto River. Around a rapid, there is a short portage across the hypotenuse at their confluence. During my walk I notice several old tent rings and *inukshuks*, the small totems of the Inuit. Now white travelers erect them too. The difference between a white-made *inukshuk* and an old one is the elaborate balancing act of the stones. Older ones are made simply from one or two stones turned vertically. *Inukshuks* are different from hunting blinds. A blind can be a large boulder, or a low wall built of rocks. The most subtle blind I've seen was in Labrador, north of Nain. I would never have seen it if my native companion hadn't pointed it out. At the edge of a beach was an outcrop of rock. In this formation was an indentation, like the corner of a room. Across its face was a skillfully built wall high enough to crouch behind. It was used to hunt seals when they came to the beach to lie in the sun.

I've never known what to do when I see white-made "canoer cairns." It's like writing "Jane was here." Last winter I met an old hand who has been traveling, writing, and photographing in the Arctic since the 1930s. I asked him what he did. He simply answered, "Why, I knock them down. Don't you?"

At a large red outcrop, I stop to see whether I could pitch my tent on top of it. There is enough flat space to sleep on. Instead of using pegs, I use rocks to secure the tent's guy lines. The view of the far hills is deepened by the evening light. I walk back down to finish unloading *Loon*.

For dinner, I set up my fly rod and walk over a hundred yards of smooth, white rocks to the eddy at the end of the rapid. I have eight feet of six-pound test monofilament for leader and a two-inch Royal Coachman streamer. The trick is to cast the red-and-white streamer beyond the shallows into the deep, rippling water. I don't have much luck. Farther downstream, in calm water, I see two fish rising. I walk toward them. Sometimes a rising fish isn't interested in anything but what it feeds on; other times it's not picky. I cast the streamer.

Stripping line in, I wonder if the streamer's plop landing scared off the fish. My thought is answered as the streamer enters the shallows. Behind the fly rises a mound of water. Something will happen. The water gets shallow. If I keep pulling in line, won't it get too shallow for the fish? If I stop pulling in the streamer to give the fish a chance to bite, will it? I keep the streamer moving slowly. The water gets shallower. The mound of water following grows until the fish's back breaks the surface. At the last possible moment, the fish takes the fly, then spins off toward deep water, the hook set.

A half hour passes before I can retrieve enough line to get the fish back in shallow water. I wade in to pick it up. On land, I quickly break its spine. This is a long fish, not fat. The head makes up one-third of its body length. These trout are under-nourished. I remove one fillet—all I can eat. Under the shadow of the red rock, I let the rest of its orange body slip out of my hand into the water where it momentarily languishes in the current and then is carried away.

The best fisherman I know is Bernie. Great gardeners have green thumbs. What great fishermen have I don't know, but I've seen it watching Bernie fish. He gets his mind out along his hand through that rod, down the line to the fly. When the fly was in the water, he wasn't looking at the landscape. On a slow day, patience seemed the difference between catching one fish and no fish. Bernie taught me that if you're going to release a fish, wet your hands before touching it. A dry hand on a fish's skin is comparable to a burn on human skin; it scars the fish and leaves it vulnerable to infection.

Fumbling in the wannigan for my fishing bag, I remembered the end of college. I was going to Ireland for the summer. In the fall I would be attending University College Cork, Ireland. Bernie was off to see a bigger piece of the world with three friends. When we left our dorm rooms, neither of us planned to meet, although we knew we'd both pass through Ireland. From Shannon Airport, it took me most of a day to reach the Dingle peninsula, first by train, then by bus, then by walking a mile in from the main road to the remote little town of Clahane. I had no more knowledge of where I was than the map told me. It was mid-June and beautiful. After finding a bed and breakfast and taking a brief nap, I went for a walk through town.

The first thing that passed me was a horse-drawn milk cart controlled by a tweed cap with a man snoozing under it. The second thing that passed me was a woman riding a bike, the type of bike and type of woman you'd see in English movies from the 1940s. The third thing that passed me was a car carrying Bernie and his friends. We embraced. We didn't comment on the billion-to-one chance of its happening. Without even asking me if I'd brought my fishing rod, Bernie said, "Let's go fishing." I did have my rod, and we inquired in the town's pub where we could fish. "You're in luck," said the man behind the bar. "The Clahane Valley has one of the best salmon rivers in the west of Ireland. It's been owned by the Lords Clahane for nine hundred years. They've taken good care to maintain it. For a modest fee, the water bailiff might let you on it."

For full effect, the seasoned publican wiped a few glasses dry before he continued. "But," he said, "you're out of luck if you want to catch salmon. They haven't come in the river yet. They're expected, but no one's caught one. It's great good luck to catch the first salmon of the season here. Usually it's the water bailiff, the priest, or the lord. They're the only ones with extra time on their hands."

We finally found the house of the water bailiff, who invited us in to look us over. "Of course, you have your own equipment?"

"Oh, yes," we said.

"And you won't be on the river longer than three days?"

"No, only one day, we just want to see which of us will catch the first salmon."

The bailiff laughed. "There's been very few fish up yet, and quite a few of us trying to catch them. No one's caught one. Have you ever fished an Irish river? Or caught a salmon?"

"No," we said.

He charged us a pound apiece to fish for a day, figuring the salmon were safe.

That night's talk in the pub revolved around the few hardy fishermen who had come early to try their hand at catching the first salmon.

Bernie nudged me. "What's the bet, Rob?"

"Let's not make it too steep," I said. "I have a feeling who's going to win. Loser buys the drinks, how's that?"

"Fair enough," said Bernie, and we staggered off to bed.

The river was a long one. Few people were fishing it. We set up our delicate, six-foot-tall bamboo trout rods, and in jeans and sneakers set out after our salmon. We didn't have a net. We separated, wishing each other luck. The last thing either of us wanted was the other fishing at his elbow. We had picked out a rendezvous far upstream for the late afternoon.

The day was bright, and a wind blew down after 1:00 P.M. from the north: two conditions that were not helping me. Brightness keeps fish below the surface and a crosswind kept my fly tangled in the gorse behind my shoulder, or reduced my good casts to a pathetic fifteen feet. Once I did get a strike or I hooked a submerged stick. In either case, I got terribly excited until it let go. By late afternoon I was wet to my knees and cold. As I walked with my mud-covered sneakers toward our rendezvous, I had some satisfaction seeing Bernie in an equally sorry state. Only when I walked right up to him did I see the beautiful twelve-pound salmon lying at his feet. I was bursting with questions. He was about to answer them when we saw a white Peugeot bumping along the side of a tract where peat was being cut. Two men got out and walked toward us. One was the water bailiff. The other was a fisherman. With no more than a nod from the bailiff, the two men crouched to look at the fish. The fisherman turned the salmon over gently, then left it to lie on its side, patting it once. "That's a nice fish. Don't tell me you both caught it."

Bernie smiled.

"We've been trying everything," said the man. "I've been

fishing every day for a week with no luck. I know every trick in the river. How did you catch it? What did you catch it on?"

"A woolly worm," replied Bernie.

"A woolly what?" said the man, exchanging a look with the water bailiff. They both leaned forward.

"A woolly worm. It's a black fuzzy thing. I tied it myself. It's supposed to resemble a caterpillar. Nothing else was working, and I know the woolly worm works on trout at home, so I gave it a try." Bernie paused, but no one had anything to say, so he continued. "I let it drift downstream and retrieved it after it was sixty degrees below me. I put it in ahead of some riffles and let it float through them, and *wham*, look what I got. I knew he was big. He almost broke my rod." Bernie gestured to the rod in the grass.

"You caught *this* on *that*?" the bailiff questioned. "First he tells us he caught the fish on a 'woolly worm' no one's ever heard of, then he tells us he caught it on that tiny rod. It's no taller than he is!"

"Extraordinary" was all the fisherman said.

Apologetically Bernie explained that it had taken him a long time to land the fish because he didn't have a net. "What type of fishing rods do you use?"

The bailiff said, "Salmon rods, nine or twelve feet tall and thick as this," he said, holding up his thumb.

They offered to drive us back into town. We didn't want to muck up their backseat, but they insisted. At the water bailiff's house Bernie showed them his fly box—as ratty a collection of chewed-up flies as you'd ever see, but they all caught fish. Bernie gave the other fisherman his woolly worm and asked him how long he'd been in Clahane.

"You might say a long time," the man said. "I'm Lord Clahane."

I smile remembering the astonishment on our faces. Since then I've given up sport fishing. I fish for food. To say it's a sport is wrong because a sport is a "contest entered into by consenting adversaries." Bulls, foxes, fish, birds, deer—no creature consents to its own torture, or death.

Leaving the rapids at the bottom of Muskox Lake, I paddle over a wide section of river, staying close to the right shore. The view has no conclusion except for a thin blue smudge where the sky meets the earth. The hills resemble the work of a sloppy water-colorist who let too much water bead up at the bottom of the sky wash. Paddling in deep water with no rapids in sight lets me appreciate how *Loon* handles. Even fully loaded she responds quickly, and picks up good speed with a few quick, powerful strokes. She glides forever and feels balanced and stable when I rock side to side.

Soon we slide through a riffle and approach a large rapid. Even without climbing a hill to look, I can tell it's big. The sharp fingers of white kicking up at the edge of the river's horizon mean a steep drop and a portage. Taking no chances, I glide with the current to a small cove above the rapid. From the top of a rise, I see it's not a rapid but a powerful chute—an immense tongue of wave ending in a tip of white foam. The mighty Back River is twenty yards wide, one solid hump of water pressed into this narrow shape. The portage is several hundred yards up a hill, across its moss-covered top, then down to the river in a zigzag course over flights of terraced stone.

Busybody that I am, I can keep track of what's occurring on each bank. I can throw a stone across most places. A hydrologist could tell me what makes the curving tongue of water move the way it does. But could he express why the light striking it just so and why the numen of this day make it so captivating? I kick these thoughts around as I portage my four loads. I have no rhythm yet. I've much adjusting to do, not only to the loads I carry, but to being alone. On my first solo trip I consulted the *I Ching* for what lay in store for me on my journey:

> *When three people journey together,*
> *Their number decreases by one.*
> *When one man journeys alone,*
> *He finds a companion.*

As I walk back from my second carry, several swallows flying low over the water touch the corner of my vision. I watch as two, then four, then six cliff swallows fly out over the water to swoop on the wind with their friends. Their wings seem like velvet.

The early afternoon follows the same vein. The river remains narrow, randomly dotted with islands. I ask *Loon* on which side should we paddle. Instead of choosing, we wind our way in and out of the islands. Occasionally a merganser or an oldsquaw breaks from the water's edge and scoots across the river in front of *Loon*.

I take an afternoon nap on shore. I still prefer to travel in the dusky night. I won't shoot rapids, or attempt difficult navigating, but on the map this section of the river looks fine for a night-paddle.

Around sunset, back on the water, I drift gently through this narrow section of river. To paddle when there's more light on the water surface than on land is an unusual sensation. The sun sets ahead, to my left, and behind me the purple sky deepens the land's darkness. I feel it might all disappear if I make too much noise. Soon my intellect surrenders. Only my eyes are here.

During these unclaimed hours the fabric of the water is a delicate color. Each wavelet savors a scoop of light-orange cadmium in its trough from the sun that doesn't quite set. Over their small, round crests lies a turquoise cloth, easier to see looking out the corner of my eye. Each time my paddle bumps the gunwale or my stroke makes a *whoosh*, I cringe.

Emil Nolde would understand this. His watercolors appear inside my head. It is said he crossed an important line in his development painting outside in winter, furiously doing watercolors of the landscape. It was snowing. Dissatisfied with each watercolor, he threw them in the snow, continuing to try to capture the feeling he wanted with the next one. Only when he gave up did he look at the wasted pieces of paper and realize how the wet snow had completed each watercolor. The snow had softened and blurred what his hand had painted, finishing each one more beautifully than the last.

My companion sounds are their *whack* of fish jumping and the subtler *swoosh* of their tails on the surface. Everything except me holds its breath, then a loon cries. It swims in the shadow of the opposite shore; a silver thread unravels in the water behind it. Sound upon sound, the cries pile up, a coloratura, then they fade among the shadows. The water, the night, hungrily swallow the sounds.

I lose track of time and how far I've traveled. I enter a wide stretch of river. The map indicates the outlet is on the far side in the north corner. I lift *Loon* and my gear over a few rocks and slip into a pond. Wait: Isn't this odd? A river the size of the Back becoming a dinky pond? I sit and stew. I've paddled several hours. It's barely light, but not dark. I couldn't have lost the river, could I?

A stone rattles down the hill behind me. I stand right up in *Loon*. Whatever it is, it's big. In the half-light, I discern a musk-ox having difficulty finding a comfortable place to sleep. Repeatedly it lies down, only to heave itself back up. The musk-ox wanders a little farther on the hillside and repeats this motion. The final effort is to throw its body sideways onto a tall clump of willows. Under its weight the willows object, snapping and scrunching. I hear its heartfelt sigh.

I climb a ridge on the opposite side of the pond. Nothing but rocks and more rocks, dark foreboding rocks, around me. I see no glint of river unrolling through them. I keep looking at the map, hoping it will provide the answer.

Time to camp. I find a circular space of hard ground big enough for the tent. It's not comfortable, but I'm not as fussy as the musk-ox.

In the morning I feel better, but the weather is gray and squally. I look around. I still don't know where the river is. Having failed the first rule of navigation, constant vigilance, I apply the second: start from what you know and go toward what you don't know. I trace last night's paddle on the map, trying to understand where I went off course. I can't figure it out. I delve into my pack for a second set of maps. I carry 1:250,000 series maps, square sheets that condense four miles to the inch. Because I'm interested in the part of the map the river flows through, to save space I cut them down and join them together, discarding most of each sheet. I get out my backup maps and see my mistake. In cutting down one square I had cut off an essential two-inch strip of the river. Now I can see the pond on the map. The real river lies into the wind, the opposite direction from where I was heading last night.

I stand on the rocks, watching the waves build, and try to decide whether to stay put or paddle. If I wait for the wind to die, the paddle will be easy, but my desire to know exactly where I am outweighs my common sense. Instead of waiting, I put the spray skirt on and set off. I tell myself that I want to see if Denny was correct about the tumblehome creating buoyancy.

Loon rides high and steady. The spray skirt throws off the rain and the occasional sloppy wave. Because I'm out of shape, and tired after last night's long paddle, my arms are soon spongy. I have three-quarters of a mile to cover directly into waves and wind. I make little progress.

I stroke forward, then rest, use the paddle to keep the bow

pointing at the proper angle to the wind and the waves, which don't always come from the same quarter. If I rest too long, *Loon* backslides and loses steerage. Paddling too hard or too long is exhausting and bound to lose more ground than it gains. The idea is to pick the opportune moments to make progress and not to lose ground resting in between.

I throw nervous glances toward the waves thrashing against the rocky weather shore. Eventually *Loon* inches under the protecting scowl of the lee shore: a high rock face. Only eddies and ruffles of wind swipe at me. I land.

These ledges are covered in thick grass. This place must get good sun. I find my first colonies of blooming daisies and small, white-flowering saxifrage.

When the weather clears in the afternoon, I walk to the point where the river's wide section narrows again. I set up my ancient fiberglass spinning rod with an equally battered Dardevle lure. If I come to a lake, or a deep fast section of the river without rapids, the odds are that a lure in the water, more than a fly, will catch fish. I don't need to eat fish because I still have most of my food, but if I save meals now by catching fish, I won't run out of other foodstuffs as quickly. I catch a trout, clean it, and fry it for dinner.

The following day, in Gold Lake, the sun returns. I weave through numerous little islands, nesting sites for different types of small birds.

Around me float a thousand chips of winking light and larger patches of deep blue—the water's reinterpretation of sun and sky. Leaving the cluster of islands, I stay in the middle of the river, enjoying a sleepy afternoon paddle. The paddling is hypnotic. I feel even slight fluctuations in light or wind. I slip into a pure moment and the magic of being on water. My thoughts stoop to consider an insect on the water, a feather. Other thoughts gallop to the horizon and feel the tug of the Arctic Ocean in the river. Inside these moments I become pure verb. I surrender.

I see half a dozen Arctic terns cavorting. Terns are birds that turn the endless task of feeding into a visual pleasure, as much an art as an essential habit. Isn't the river a two-way platter, serving terns on its surface and fish from below? For their devotion, and wise investment in water, the river gives good returns. Each species finishes its life near water, having earned a place in the river's heart.

As I round a bend a speck of yellow brings me back from my word games: a Caterpillar tractor. I come to the remains of a mining exploration camp. Vaguely I remember seeing the tractor when I was here in 1976 with Bernie. Old barrel labels indicate that a mining company called Cominco established this camp, and one called Silverhart now owns it. I can confirm this in the land records office in Yellowknife. Either the companies are coming back, or they don't give a damn about what they left behind: food containers, fuel drums, plastic bags, tin cans, beer cans, expended shotgun shells, a tractor, cabin frames, rusty nails, broken glass, a dock, and two broken aluminum boats. For more than twelve years their stuff has been awaiting their return.

There's a law against mining companies leaving trash behind, but it's hard to police every camp. A loophole exempts company camps created before the law was passed. Cominco is a successful company. Silverhart might be more a paper stock company than a solid concern, but even so it ought to clean up its mess.

I discover the outcome of their labor in row upon row, rack upon rack of core samples. The scattered rocks, the spilled trays, and the fragmented pieces are now a splintered library, trashed and broken. Over time, people with other interests come wanting the wooden trays for a fire, the nails for a project. They tip out the core samples to get what they need. Perhaps one winter the ice shifted a rack, spilling its contents. Now they are pieces of a geological hash no one can unravel.

I am sure Cominco takes pride in how it treats its employees and equal pride in how it serves its investors. As great a benefit will accrue when companies like Cominco actively care for the land too. A small shift, a world of difference. With a crew of four and Cominco's help, in two weeks I could clean this mess up.

I am angry. But have I a right to be? This is a multiple-use area. Miners have as much right here as I do.

I paddle hard to escape. Miles farther, I calm down. Then I see two old, rusted fuel barrels on the bank, half a mile apart. Ice and high water have lifted them from the mining camp and brought them downriver.

At night I write a letter to both companies, a letter I will mail when I get home.*

I can't believe my good luck. Every night it's clear and light. My mind is settling down. A rhythm is developing on the water and in camp, a rhythm that frees me to notice things I haven't seen before. My dreams are more potent. I remember them all day long. I am aware of my body in ways I've never experienced it before. I remember people and events I haven't thought about for years.

Approaching Malley Rapids, as if taking a breath, the landscape steps back from the river. The hills in the distance resemble views in Ireland and Scotland. Rocks lie scattered along the sides of the river like game pieces that slipped unnoticed out of a giant's bag. Days pass. I paddle. I camp. I walk in the evening light over the tundra, or I walk in the daytime and paddle in the evening. The hours in the day run according to the weather and my stomach.

Before Malley Rapids I portage around a short, tough section

---

*A reply to my letter arrived in November 1989. The manager of Cominco Mines, Inc., Western Canada, wrote to acknowledge receipt of my letter and to express his love of the North too.

of river. I see a mouse tail disappear into a crevice. In the manner of Captain Back, I name the rapid Mouse Tail Rapid.

Captain Back named everything after important expedition patrons or members of his team. Approaching this rapid, Malley, his manservant, was lost for several hours. When he finally sloshed into camp, I doubt whether the gibing and ridicule from the rest of the crew diminished his thankfulness at having found them again. To commemorate the event, Captain Back named the rapid after him.

Inuit names for places have not survived, but they often had a specific, practical application. For example, the name for the Back River was Thlew-ee-choh, or the Great Fish River.

I turn a bend and see miles of wide open water, no rapid yet, and a good current to piggyback on. I stop paddling, even steering, to see what happens. Instead of a canoe loaded with intent, *Loon* becomes a piece of the river's flotsam, slowly arching to the left, a white-and-black wooden feather carrying me along. There is no wind to play with the silence. The water is glass. I drift past a sandy island. Several terns start up but share my lackadaisical mood. After one or two halfhearted dives at my hat, they retreat. When the word "grace" was invented, part of the image must have been of a tern flying.

I watch the light-green tassels of weeds wavering on the river bottom. As I pass the end of the island, a sudden explosion catches me off guard. My hands grab the gunwales. *Loon* rocks. Next to me a white swan erupts into flight. Once airborne, it settles down to skim over the water. I relax. I watch. The two wingtips together, on their downbeat, seem to touch the river. As the swan recedes it loses shape, but the white body against the dark mass of water and land remains visible for miles ahead.

I hear Malley Rapids before I see them. Just above them, the river turns right. I round the corner and beach *Loon*. Slabs of rock jut out of the earth, others lie on their sides. They look like dancers' bodies, frozen into various shapes. I perceive a free-form Stonehenge.

The face of each rock is black with lichens, a severe contrast to the pink, flesh-colored granite in the rapid. I puzzle over this difference until I realize the land rocks would be pink too if they were scrubbed as regularly as the ones in the water; the water, and early each year the ice, keep their surfaces lichen free.

This is the same pink granite that forms the northeast coast of New England. It reminds me of Singing Beach at home, a gentle arch of sand bookended by two pink granite headlands. They bend the beach between them. The beach gets its name from the fine sand that squeaks when you scuffle it. I grew up on that beach, and grew up day-sailing that coastline with my father. From Marblehead, to Rockport, out to Minot's Light, to Egg Rock, it's the same granite.

In *Loon*, I scuttle down the first part of Malley Rapids staying close to the right shore. The second half is trickier. If I stand on shore, I can edge the canoe up to the ledge. Then I use the sternline to slide it over, and pull it back inshore. I can balance on the gunwales with my hands and jump in, or I can portage and be safe. I've never jumped into a canoe before, so I try it. And it works.

In the runoff horsetails, I let the strong current push me along before I begin paddling. The paddle blade slices into the water over and over again.

I see my dad at the head of the table, carving a roast, offering more gravy, asking if everyone has enough. Carving is a specialty of his. He's used a particular bone-handled knife for as long as I can remember. He stands off to the side of the table working the knife in his right hand, holding the sharpening steel in his left— the way a grasshopper works its back legs—away from the table so the steel filings won't fall in the meat. Once someone gave him an electric carver. He tried it, then quietly put it away.

Often he ran the dinner table like a meeting, asking in turn each of the five children what he or she had done that day. Private conversations were not well received. In the sixties my brother brought home a copy of the militant Black Panther newsletter thinking that would be a good dinner table topic. It wasn't. As he did that night, my father can hit the table and have everything, and everyone, jump in place.

Nothing pleases him more than to sit in his den smoking a pipe, a fire going, browsing a nautical book or doing needlepoint. His den is a small, octagonal room. From the brick fireplace, two andirons in the shape of owls face you, black as the bricks inside the fireplace. Little glass, ceramic, and bronze owls perch about the room, recalling his father's farm, "Owl's Nest." On the walls are etchings by a western artist named Boreen: scenes of cowboys, western mesas, bucking broncos. My mother cleans this room, but she has the sense not to move anything around, least of all his sixty-three pipes.

The mantel is crowded with photographs of his and other people's boats. There is a couch, his desk, and three chairs, one covered in black leather held down with those bumpheaded brass tacks that feel cool to the touch.

There are seven chiming clocks throughout the house. Every Saturday, he winds each one, except the pendulum clock. From where he sits in the den he can hear if they strike in unison or not. He's a happy man when they do. He makes a mental note of the speedy or reluctant timepiece if they don't.

I hear geese calling. Caught unaware close to shore, they scramble overland among the gray rocks to escape me. They're molting and can't fly. After Malley Rapids, the river opens its gauge.

There was something gathering around my father during the six months before he entered the hospital. No one could put a finger on it, but in the evenings, after his normal quota of a cocktail and its dividend, he would act as if he were in a boxing ring, bobbing and weaving, fighting some invisible opponent, determined not to quit.

I've grown up in the middle. Out of five children, I'm the third. Of the three men in the family, I'm the one in the middle again, between my father and my younger brother, Tom. Being the middle tended to keep me quiet, at least growing up. I could see both sides of an argument. I felt the force of feelings. I envy people like my father who seem as clear and directed as arrows. He was born during the First World War and fought in the Second. He sees the middle ground as something to pass over. I stayed in the middle with my own feelings, deep and felt, but not expressed.

Late one Saturday night we watched a science-fiction film on television called *The Eggplant from Outer Space,* or something equally illuminating. I could hear the ice cubes rattle each time he raised his glass. He wanted to talk to me. I wanted to talk to him, but neither of us was willing to speak.

I finish the day paddling late into the evening. Tired but happy as I set up camp, I say out loud, "Our Father who art in Heaven."

I hope he isn't.

JULY 19

The next day for breakfast, I eat the last of my Familia mixed with hot water. Another cup of coffee and I'm off. Paddling all morning brings me to a rapid that slants to the left with high banks on either side. On the map two parallel bars across the river and an *R* at the side indicate a rapid to watch out for. I beach *Loon* on the river's inside curve and set out toward the loud roar to scout the rapid. I walk and hop on cream-colored and taffy-brown rocks until I'm held up by a chirp. I stop. As if to prevent my taking more forward steps, I hear it again. "Chirripp." Out on a rock steps a brown fuzzy ball of a bird. With all the commanding presence of Moses returning from the mountain, it chirrups again. I dare go no farther, though I see its chirp is one of fear. An intrepid juvenile plover stands on the rock in front of me, as tall as a toothpick. Tiny not-yet-wings stick out from its sides. Its distinctive black bill and quizzical eye mark it for a life of adventure and long-distance flight. Is this another summer orphan? Both of us think, "Where is Mother?" The tiny plover had little to fear from me, although a gull, a jaeger, an owl, a weasel, a wolf wouldn't give a thought before gobbling it up. The Victorian world's passion for plover on toast was strong enough to reduce the endless migratory flocks to a handful. If there's a dollar to be made on killing, we'll turn it into a science.

More to the point are the consequences the chick will suffer for having broken the one golden plover rule its mother laid down: when I put you somewhere, DON'T MOVE. I had forced it to break the rule by scouting the rapids. The young plover flees. I break one of my rules, don't intrude, and follow it.

By the time it's traveled ten yards toward cover, I can tell it feels it's crossed the Alps and the Atlantic, all on foot. It reaches the cover of grass and heads for the safety of a willow patch. As it enters the willow clump it glances back and trips on the edge of a leaf. Over it tumbles, the momentum spilling it headfirst and sideways into the bush. I turn away wondering, If this plover grows up, will this moment have a special place in its memory? Will it remember this as it sails over international borders, great lakes, and tropical forests during its migratory flight between the Arctic and the South American pampas?

When I'm back in the canoe and about to push out into the rapid, mother plover arrives. She's frantic. She goes from rock to rock, gravel patch to grassy knoll, calling, calling, calling for her chick. She couldn't care less about my presence. The loud roar of the rapid obscures her call. The young plover's answering cry would be even harder for her to hear. I could show her the exact willow clump where the little one cowers, but she'd never understand. Saddened, I leave before knowing the outcome.

The rapid is a slalom, first curving left, then arcing to the right. From the high bank, I had picked out a few major water marks and now am trying to find them, but everything changes in a rapid. What appears calm water and easy going can turn into chaos. What looks impossible from land reveals an opening from the water. This is fun, a series of Vs to aim for, some quick sideways ferrying, a back-paddle; then more of the same. Vs are created by rocks close to or above the water surface, channeling a piece of the river between them. Often a V indicates deep water and a safe passage between the rocks. This rapid goes on for a mile. I stay in it the whole way, using my knees to guide *Loon*, planting them wide apart, leaning weight on them to accelerate the canoe's turns.

Coming through the last horserace, I tap *Loon* on the side with the paddle, as a thank you.

In the afternoon five jaegers join me, working their beat. "Jaeger" is German for "hunter," and they deserve the name. Their presence, the swoop and glide of their dark bodies, their sinister hovering and the calmness with which they strike are unlike any other bird. A tern may be an avid hunter, but its playfulness and grace make it appear friendly. I rarely see jaegers alone; they hunt in packs, or pairs. One will swing in from the river and sweep low over a bank. If anything, scared by the first bird's shadow, scurries toward a safer location, the second jaeger kills it.

There's an undeniable beauty in the dark-gray bird with its small head, dark cap, white breast, and long, pencil-thin tail. The casual ease with which it flies is a visible mastery, a slow grace accompanying a deadly skill.

I begin computing distances and days. I'm not behind but I should pick up the pace. I've been traveling twenty-eight days. I want to reach the bottom of Beechey Lake while this good weather lasts. Beechey is a long, thin lake, the river's hairpin turn to the southeast.

I camp on the squishy goose grass uncovered by the dwindling river. I've climbed a small clay dome above the tent where I can see up and down the river. As if a child tugged on my pant leg, a small breeze competes for my attention, rustling the pages of my journal. At least it keeps the mosquitoes occupied. They have to try harder for a landing place. Once they land, they're tenacious, patient prospectors, walking across what must seem to them acres of me, feeling for an opening with their blind probe. On a sweater, or something with a loose weave, they resemble the small bobbing oil rigs I've seen down south. On skin, they seem picky (unlike the devilish black fly), forever fiddling around for the right spot. For something that can inflict sharp pain, they're delicately built the slightest touch knocks them out of kilter. I can hold one down by a leg and it will move away leaving its leg under my finger. Mosquitoes can't crawl into things and up things, the way black flies do. They need lots of clearance to walk on their six long legs up a cuff or a sleeve, not like those bastard black flies that welcome the challenge of a tight squeeze.

Another difference between them is that mosquitoes slip their snouts in and suck whereas black flies actually take a bite. If they can, other black flies bite the same raw area, increasing their frenzy and my misery. The corners of eyes are a favored place. In another week or so, when they emerge, I'll never be able to sit out as I do today.

One side of the rock I lean against has vibrant green grass around it, a contrast to the dull land color where the ground squirrels have made their network of tunnels. Bird droppings add nutrients to the soil, providing good footing for the grass. The dens of bears, foxes, wolves, and wolverines are dressed in this green skirt. I've seen a bear shoveling its way into a colony, uprooting yards of similar bank in a few scoops, sweeping up ground squirrels like popcorn. If there's one thing I would never wish to be, it's a ground squirrel trapped at the end of its tunnel as the bear starts digging.

While sitting here, I'm watching swimming practice for a brood of seven young mergansers and their mother in the fast water upriver from the tent. They've been in the same spot for an hour, the chicks in a line behind her. If her body weren't in the lead, they would be swept away in the strong current. As it is, they struggle. Once in a while, she'll zigzag, and they have to scurry to get back in behind her. The chicks are constantly grabbing bugs as they sweep past on the current. One chick breaks formation to hydroplane to more attractive bugs beyond its reach. Each time it loses its place, it fights to get back to the end of the line. From there it begins pushing up the line to get closest to mother. Before reaching the head of the line, it sees another bug and loses its place again. I know some people like that.

The shadow of the rock stretches out and swings across me as the sun's angle lowers. Time to turn in.

I force myself up at 3:00 A.M. Outside the light is just gathering. I don't finish my breakfast (two cups of coffee and some Cream of Wheat) and rolling my pack until 5:00 A.M. That's slow, but loading the canoe is now second nature. The wannigan goes alongside the midthwart on the bow side, with the two camera cases in front of it. My personal pack fits behind my seat. To balance my weight in the stern, the heavy food pack goes farthest forward. The extra paddles and the fishing rod case slip in forward of the midthwart. If there are rapids, and there will be today, I tie the paddles and rod case in. The light-blue spray skirt goes on last.

To avoid losing anything if they tip over, some people tie everything into the canoe, and they criticize me for not doing it. Perhaps they won't lose anything, but tying everything in also creates an opportunity for losing everything. Upturned and full of water, a canoe is an unwieldy object. A fully loaded canoe with everything securely tied in is a lethal weapon. The added weight of sodden gear, dangling appendages of partly tied-in stuff worked loose by smashing rocks and the water's force, make it impossible to manage—may even cause it to become stuck on rocks far from shore. The thought of a waterlogged, fully loaded canoe driving my leg or chest against the upriver side of a rock makes me want to take my chances with an empty, more manageable canoe, nudging and swimming it to shallow water. There I can flip it right side up. If I have a paddle tied in I can pick up my gear. Even if I don't find it all, I still have the canoe, my transportation to safety.

The sun is a hot white spotlight working warmth into my shoulders and back, and I make excellent miles all morning. I'm not far from Beechey Lake. Taking a break on the water, I set the stove up on the canoe's bottom, out of the wind, to brew coffee. Lunch is two handfuls of cheese and raisins, plenty of clear, cold, sweet-tasting Back River water, and coffee drunk from my wooden bowl.

By the late afternoon I've made over thirty miles. Helped by the strong current, I start to hurry. When I reach Beechey Lake, if it's calm, I might travel a short distance down it.

I shoot easy-looking rapids without scouting them—two little ones, then a third. The first two Vs guide *Loon* to the right approach for descent; they are easy. I stand up as I approach the third V for a final check, leaving myself enough distance to alter course if needed. The first two rapids have lulled me into a state of inattention. The third looks calm: I see a healthy V to the left of a large rock that stands out of the water halfway across the river. The far left side of the river has a mare's tails kicking up, sharp spumes of white water. I don't want to be near them. The current swings *Loon* into position to enter the V by the large rocks. I see another possible route to the right, closer to shore, but it appears rockier.

Twenty yards out, I drift toward the V. Habit, sheer habit in preferring to shoot rapids close to shore, changes my mind. I go for the route closer to land. I don't get off scot-free. Like the fox who looks back as it finishes crossing thin ice, I, too, get wet. I could not have seen the sharp drop that runs the length of the river unless I had walked below the rapid. The upper lip of the drop blends in with the calm water farther on, giving the impression of nothing spectacular. On its own, a four-foot drop isn't dramatic, but add to it a strong current, an unsuspecting canoeist in a loaded canoe, sailing blind over the drop into a hidden rock, with a circling eddy underneath, and a standing wave to bat him around. That's disaster.

I see the drop as I go over it. The funny thing is I have the movie camera running. I thought these rapids would be safe to film in. I wonder what the film will show.

I shoot blind over the drop, three seconds and it's over. I fly between two rocks, heading toward a third. I go straight into it. The rock holds me, then, like a weight lifter, boosts *Loon*'s bow up. The stern goes down. I hate the sound of a canoe cracking against rock, especially if it's caused by my own stupidity. I stop paddling, hands on the gunwales, and wait. A spasm of fear flows through me equal to the force of the water. *Loon* slips off to the left. The rock scrapes along the whole side of the canoe, a granite fingernail on a fragile blackboard. I get to shore, unload everything, empty the water, and stand on firm land looking back at the rapid. It flows by indifferently, as if nothing had ever happened.

All I wish for is some straight-ahead paddling, no rapids, no excitement. Chris told me to film lots of rapids, tough ones. He got his wish. I won't do that again, ever. I'm self-conscious enough in front of the camera without having to run it in rapids where every ounce of energy is focused—my hands, my heart, my eyes, my mind—on navigating safely through the rocks, away from the force of waves and the slap of back eddies.

On my drive from Boston to Yellowknife, I stopped at the canoeing arm of Outward Bound in Minnesota. I'm a friend of the current director's wife, and although they would not be there, they had said that staff orientation would be in progress and to make myself at home in back of their cabin.

I was curious to see the reaction of top-notch paddlers to *Loon*. Because most people who had seen her weren't canoeists, *Loon* had been severely underpraised. I was proud of Denny's work. I thought people here would appreciate his craftsmanship. But during my three-day visit no one stopped to look at her, feel her weight, or even comment.

On my last day I saw a group of six canoes playing in the one rooster tail in the river behind the camp. Each canoe waited its turn, then entered the full force of the downward-rushing water to practice powerstroking and bowman sidestrokes. I yelled from shore to ask if I could play. They motioned me ahead. I portaged *Loon* to the top of the small rapid. This would be our first rapid—with an audience, no less. After I signaled that I was ready, they signaled back with a raised paddle to come ahead. I let *Loon* drift in toward the rooster tail. It would be easy if I hit the angle right. *Loon* went through in fine form. I cut out of the runoff to the opposite side of the rooster tail from where the other canoes floated and drifted in the eddy, feeling proud. I thought about what lay in store for us in the tundra. After a huddle, one of the instructor canoes detached and paddled over.

The Outward Bound canoes were made of plastic. Besides a life vest and a helmet, each instructor wielded a laminated wood paddle, or an equally indestructible metal-shaft one. I thought about what type of attitude indestructible equipment would generate in someone. Or the type of attitude developed toward water when one feels one's equipment can overpower it. I grew up in wood and canvas canoes. At the end of each day the sternman's penance was to inspect the canoe's bottom for small and large tears and then to fix them. In delicate canoes like those, a paddler learns to be sensitive to where the rocks are, to read water. Where I learned they had no spray covers or life jackets, let alone helmets. I was lucky to have had a Cree Indian guide, and the right to fail.

Just as I was feeling superior in my nostalgia, the centaur canoe arrived. In the bow, the female instructor smiled as she glided past, allowing the male instructor in the stern to come alongside me. He held our two gunwales together with his hand while he spoke.

"That's a pretty delicate canoe you have there, and that's very rough water," he said, nodding toward the small rooster tail. "There's rougher water than that around here. I'd advise you not to go into the Quetico Wilderness with that canoe. You might get hurt."

Those were fighting words and I almost rose to the bait. I thought about what I could say: "What I'm doing this summer makes the Quetico Wilderness look like a duck pond." Instead I looked at him and promised I wouldn't.

Here I am in the Northwest Territories, on its toughest river, half a day from Beechey Lake, looking at a muskox. I laid down the paddle. Talk about evolution, or lack of it. The muskox stands in a wide open area, not seeing me. The light is golden, slanting. Why not film it? I can't tip the canoe over doing that. After beaching *Loon*, I play the game Red Light, Green Light as I approach it. Each time the muskox's head swivels in my direction, I freeze. All I need is to get close and take some footage. I need to get close because if you don't with the hand-held wide-angle camera, a muskox looks like a tiny fly on film. For encouragement, I tell myself they're sweet-natured herbivores. It looks awfully close. It will show up now, won't it? Maybe not. If they charge they say you should stand still. They say muskox swerve off to the side at the last moment. Who are "they," anyway?

I move closer.

Out of the corner of my eye, I see a gull sitting comfortably on a rock, watching. Gulls don't choose sides. They're happy picking anybody's bones. I couldn't help feeling it hoped the muskox might gore me. Then it would get to sample the meat of this odd, two-legged creature.

The muskox sees me: it doesn't seem concerned and goes

on grazing. Why shouldn't it? Muskox are king here, say some natives. If attacked, a muskox can defeat a bear with the power in its shoulders, the power behind its horns, its hooves. Instead of fighting, muskox usually choose to use their speed. Defensive and peaceful: I like it that those characteristics reign in the tundra.

The muskox's cinnamon-colored hair is long and matted, like dreadlocks. Two waves of bone flow from the center of its head, down each side of its face, curving outward into sharp, tapered horns below its jawline. Where it would begin to curve up, I see its right horn is broken off. I am within twenty feet. As it's watching me, why pretend to hide?

The muskox brushes its head along the side of its white foreleg. Does it itch? Is it telling me something? The muskox is not backing away. I stop. I stand fifteen feet from it. I take five quick steps to the left. The muskox charges.

Holding on to the camera, I stumble, trip, and fall backward. When I can look up, the muskox is setting a record in the hundred-yard dash, already almost out of sight, having run past me.

For a man whose goal is to observe wildlife and not disturb it, I've made a mess. I've ruined my friend's breakfast, upset my own stomach, only to realize the lens cap is still on. The gull sits undisturbed, although it looks disappointed. Filming is going to be more complicated than I thought.

I make an uneventful entrance into Beechey Lake. It's late afternoon. The mountains on the far side are awash in purple-blue distance. There's a light breeze blowing down the lake. The sun has dimmed to a red disk gently resting on the horizon. I paddle the south shore awhile, then cross the lake, arriving at a point where several unusual *inukshuks* can be seen from the water. They are lined up in a row, pointing down the lake. Are they merely direction markers? I decide to have dinner with them and to film them too—a pleasure compared to the rest of my day's cinematographic efforts. More than once, Captain Back mentions seeing three standing stones indicating a direction or an astronomical sight. An astronomical sight would be wonderful. It would add to the mystery of this place.

Dinner over, I sit down to begin an idea, one that has been brewing in me for several days. My eight-year-old nephew, Marshall, asked me to write him a letter from the tundra. What if I make him an alphabet instead? An illustrated ABC of summer thoughts. I'll call it a Tundra Alphabet—better yet, a Tundrabet. I'll write each letter as I think of it. I'll start with his initial.

M *is for Marshall, also for muskox.*

Let me tell Marshall about muskox. If you haven't seen one, you wouldn't believe they exist. They seem out of a myth. Nietzsche tells us how the gods killed themselves when one of their number claimed there could be only one god, and one god only: they died laughing. Science and monotheism have driven the gods from Olympus, but not the muskox from the Arctic. In about four centuries, the church and the telescope changed the world's viewpoint. Now science controls people's lives. The technician is the modern missionary bringing every bird, every grass blade, wave pattern, and molecule into the fold of human knowledge and domination. Everything under the sun and beyond is fair game. As we continue to unfurl our presence on earth, must everything have a name and a use?

At Beechey Lake, the river takes a decided southeast turn, which dampened Captain Back's spirits. If it continued this way, he was afraid the Great Fish River would flow into Hudson Bay and defeat his purpose of finding a passage into the Arctic Ocean to map unknown coastline. The unraveling of the mysteries of the Great Fish River was incidental for Back, a warm-up for his work at the coast.

I can't wait to reach the foot of the lake. Even after a long day and dinner I start down the lake toward one of the blue finger points ahead. The sun, still balanced close to the horizon, is a deep rich orange. Through the evening, clouds roll onto the lake, filling in the blue sky and dimming the light. A stiff breeze and an ugly gray front bullies its way in. I paddle for cover. I put an extra rock on overturned *Loon*. I go to sleep listening to the building power of the wind.

During the night it shifts 180 degrees, forcing me to relocate, a task I don't relish carrying out in just my underwear and boots. First, I have to find the new location: a hundred yards in from the shore with a solid rock wall between me and the wind. Then I have to move the dome-shaped tent. I unpeg it without collapsing it, holding the long guy ropes in my hand. When I pull out the last tent peg, we sail inland, I as the sea anchor, awkwardly following the tent, hoping not to trip. Finally I set it up again in the lee of the rocks. If the tent had touched the ground, my momentum and the wind would have simply broken the tent poles and ripped the fabric. It was stupid to have risked it. I retrieve my other stuff and drag it to the tent's new location. There is nothing to do but wait it out and try to stay dry as the rain begins.

The rain continues. Today I'm stuck in the tent. Stuck on Beechey Lake. Stuck with a sour mood.

When Bernie and I paddled down this lake, a white wolf followed us. It wove its way in and out of the rocks, a white thread sewn through the green land, effortlessly keeping up. We'd lose it among the folds in the landscape only to find it again abreast of us miles down the lake.

I spend the next day reading *The Hunchback of Notre Dame.* I immerse myself in eighteenth-century Paris, cheer with the crowds and weep with the hunchback. I think of Charles Laughton playing the movie role of Quasimodo, the hunchback, and I wish Esmeralda wasn't such a foolish woman. To dream about it all is a good rainy-day activity. There is nothing more exotic in the tundra than a French novel. The thicker, the more descriptive, the more I like them. When I first brought paperbacks on trips, I tore out each page as I read it to use as fire starters. Now I save favorite passages to reread before I burn them.

The storm blows out during the next night, and the following day is sunny. Cottonball clouds dot the blue sky. Everything glistens after the rain. I pack up. The light breeze encourages me to try sailing. With the camera tripod in the boat on full extension, I drape my yellow tarp around it and attach the Cruising Club of America pennant to the makeshift mast and sail off. I end up paddling much of the way. I film my sail, though, making remarks about Ratty and Mole and how nice it is messing about in boats. That and the pennant ought to bring a smile to the old man's face, if he sees it.

As soon as the wind quarters, I take the sail down and paddle the few remaining miles into the lake's toe, arriving in late afternoon. During the day, the clouds elongate and pile up like loaves of French bread. I feel like I'm traveling in a painting by René Magritte.

The portage at the end of Beechey Lake is around a three-quarter-mile cascade. The map indicates the portage is a mile and a half, depending on how I walk it. I choose to go slowly. I have all night.

When Captain Back arrived here his boat was too heavy and cumbersome to portage, so his crew shot the cascade. Back's journal says he left a cache here, one he never mentions retrieving on the homeward journey. In it was a spare oar. If I have time after I'm done portaging, I'll have a look for the oar.

II.

CURIOUS CREATURE

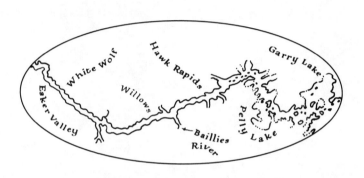

JULY 24–AUGUST 11, 1987

U *is for ugly.*

All the way on the drive north, no one—the gas station attendant, the restaurant people—no one said "boo" about *Loon*. It was as if she were an invisible ugly duckling, but in the tundra she turned into a swan.

By the time I finish the Beechey Lake portage, I can barely breathe, walk, or think. I carry three loads of sixty pounds and the fourth, the wannigan, seventy pounds, over a mile and a half, not to mention the two camera cases weighing twenty-five pounds each. I carry them as briefcases, one with each pack. The total distance is four mile-and-a-half carries with a load and three walks back for the next load, or ten and a half miles of walking. After a while it's no fun.

At the foot of Beechey, the river bends so I stay on high ground, to save time. The bank is sloppy walking, full of women's heads, as the Indians called the tufts of knotty grass growing in the wettest places. Prime ankle-twisting terrain. Having found the end of the portage on my first carry, I return over a more direct route, and pick out a few landmarks to follow with my next load. With no trees in the tundra, portaging should be a simple matter, but I've often walked myself out of the way into some dead-end quagmire. The constant temptation, especially when tired, is to try shortcuts across wetland instead of taking the time to go around it or to leave a serpentine ridge with solid footing to cross sand or bog.

I take *Loon* next. A canoe looks like an awkward thing to carry, and it can be in a wind or on an incline. Tonight in this golden liquid light, it is a pleasure. The low sun plays with my shadow, throwing it out to the side, changing *Loon* and myself into fantastic black cutouts projected against the landscape. My shadow legs stretch like rubber bands, while *Loon's* banana shape, inverted on my head, resembles an impossible millinery mobile. I think of the work of an Italian sculptor whose figures are thin and tall like my shadow. Passing a hillside, the shadow scrunches up and rushes toward me as if to whisper a secret. *Loon* and I play shadow games until the back side of the portage where the steep incline forces me to slide the canoe's weight forward, putting strain on my arms and shoulders. The midthwart bites into the back of my neck. Although I'm tempted, I can't descend straight downhill. I weave back and forth, as a skier would traverse a slope. When I lay the canoe down, the noise of the river is overwhelming. Even a hundred yards beyond the end of the cascade, the water is still aboil. Leaving *Loon* beside the pack, I return for the next item.

As I leave the hill's crest behind, the water's roar diminishes until I lose it completely. For the second time I cross too near a plover's nest for her comfort. She wings out to meet me and tries to lure me away by feigning injury. Part of the walk is over swirls of hard-packed clay pans. I see worn tracks of a mother caribou and her baby crossing in several directions. Soon more wind and rain will melt them completely away. What doesn't disappear as fast here are the bones. My eyes constantly flick back and forth between the ground at my feet and wider views. I'm walking toward a scattering of rocks on the brow of a hill that marks the beginning of the descent toward the water and the rest of my gear. The sun's light strikes one large rock, turning it into a red-gold nugget. I aim for that.

It's quiet walking. Sometimes I forget the difference between carrying on a conversation in my head and speaking out loud. When I film, I have to talk, otherwise no one would know what I was doing. But the real experience is hearing: the sound of my foot on the moss, the plover's piping, the wind's subtle range of tones, the raucous geese, the thousands of tiny wing sounds, the sound of feathers, rain. In a film, these sounds need a human interpreter.

I reach the light-drenched rock and begin a crablike descent to the shore, edging along a gentle grade around a tangle of low willows and water. At the edge of the bank where it drops to meet the river are the remains of an old hunting camp. Bones from a hundred caribou lie in the grass. I trip on a piece of half-buried wire.

Two loads done, two to go. The wannigan's next. When I took the first load, I set up the camera on the tripod with the sun behind it. I filmed a group portrait of myself and my friends: the two packs, the canoe, the wannigan. I thought I'd record how I deteriorate over the evening, filming each departure with a load on my back. Here goes.

My arms and neck are already tired. I have to keep my hands on the tumpline. I struggle against a constant urge to stop and rest. Occasional breaks to set the wannigan on a high rock are fine, but resting means having to start over. It's a tossup between continuing and having to lift the wannigan all over again. I try to forget what I'm doing. I concentrate on my feet, my breathing, but sooner or later I'm forced to think about the weight on my back.

I try going to the movies. I replay *Woman of the Year* starring Katharine Hepburn and Spencer Tracy. She's the sophisticated social columnist named Tess Harding. He's a loud, uncouth sports writer with a heart of gold working for the same newspaper. I can't remember his movie name. I describe to the wannigan the outrageous clothes Tess wears throughout the film, especially the ones she wears to the press box at the baseball game: a blouse with a short jacket and a skirt with matching hat and gloves. What makes it an unusual outfit, even in black and white, are the checks that cover the clothes, large as the squares in a bad-minton net. The squares even cover the hat and gloves!

They fall in love. They have a hard time after marriage, as she's very independent, but they get back together in the end. In the final scene Hepburn, trying to be a good wife, cooks breakfast. The toast is burned, the eggs are hard-boiled, the waffle iron explodes.

I begin the second feature, the 1937 *Lost Horizon*. Robert Conroy, aspiring world leader, is abducted to Shangri-La along with his brother and a planeload of other characters as they escape an uprising in China. The film has two details I like: one is how newspaper headlines whirl up in front of the screen and then stop, landing right side up. The second detail occurs in the dovecote where the hero and heroine are getting to know each other. She attaches small flutes to the legs of the doves that make an alluring sound as they fly.

More than on the first two carries, I notice an increase in bugs. Because my hands are on the tumpline the bugs are harder to brush off my face and the backs of my hands. I sweated off the bug dope long ago. I stop to put on more. There's definitely a rise in the level of black flies. Setting down the heavy wannigan that's been on my back for a long time creates a rising sensation, a light-headedness: the landscape becomes watery, then settles down. I don't move fast with seventy pounds on my back; one step at a time. I'll flip the tump from my forehead to a harness position across the front of my shoulders and chest, letting my neck rest. I think about eating freeze-dried food and carrying a lighter pack. But I like my box and the rice and beans it carries.

I pass the worried mother plover who must think I'm moving in. Finally I arrive at the bank. I throw the wannigan off my back and limp to the river for a drink. One more pack to carry. Aren't I clever, I think, to save the lightest load for last.

The setting sun extends the last rays to backlight the cascade and sends its light along the thin horizon, a simmering blood red. As I walk, I watch columns of mist rise off the water. Even though the black flies are aggressive, and my whole body aches, I can still croak, "How nice."

On one of the countless sections of trail made primarily by the caribou, I pick up the small body of a dead sparrow. Only the eyes are gone, death's first choice. Such small birds in such a large space; but their song can fill up a valley. Their constant chatter knits everything together. They flit up in the low grass and willows in an arc, to disappear again, the way flying fish in the ocean leap before the bow of a boat.

Ten steps farther I realize those are not columns of mist rising: they are columns of bugs. Not just any bugs—black flies. Each column is as fat around as a huge oak tree and twenty feet tall. I have no headnet, only my toque. At least the flaps will keep them out of my ears. I walk faster to get to my last load. Unfortunately a healthy number of black flies are there to greet me, swarming on my pack. Even before getting to the old hunting camp, I hear them sharpening their pincers. I throw on the pack, blather for a second in front of the camera, collapse the tripod, and take off. Anyone watching me cross the portage for the last time would have seen a biblical tower four feet wide, seven feet tall, whirling across the tundra. Had I fallen, they would not have let up, not until I was sucked dry. I remember having thought

I might look for Captain Back's oar. If there was an oar down by the river once, it's not there now. Generations of these bastards must have whittled it into toothpicks after consuming the likes of me.

I try doing everything fast but nothing is fast enough. The portage takes forever. Setting the tent up on the rocks takes forever. Getting a pot of water—everything takes too long. Every second the black flies are there batting, biting, buzzing. I open the wannigan, they're in it. They're in the tent. They're in my pockets. It's a sandstorm, except these grains want my blood.

Finally secure in the tent, I begin the slaughter. I run my palm up and down the mosquito netting at the door of the tent, ten times, twenty, and their corpses pile up at the bottom. I have to apply pressure. The body of a black fly is resilient. They take a lot of killing. Then comes the reconnaissance into the corners, the edges, my clothes. Even after twenty minutes, pockets of guerrilla black flies swarm out to attack. I laugh out loud thinking of my Inuit friend saying, "What bugs?" Their batting sound on the tent is like the sound of a heavy downpour. To end the nightmare, I fill my sister Flo's present of a small shotglass with Glenfiddich. I fill it again to toast the spirit of Mr. Bunting. I drink to the health of my worthy adversaries and wish them godspeed to their Black Fly Valhalla.

Individuality isn't something readily noticeable in the smaller winged species. Rocks, animals, medium-size birds, and up have discernible characters. Black flies, mosquitoes, all look alike, although I'm sure there must be a black fly equivalent to Jack London's White Fang. Even the Inuit have nothing good to say about them. Along with the declining level of Glenfiddich in the bottle, the level of my thinking dwindles into sleep.

The next day I wake up, roll over, and return to sleep. Black flies don't like excessive heat. The hottest part of the afternoon will dampen their activity. All I hope for is enough time to get on the water. Black flies and mosquitoes don't wait for their victims offshore. They tag along in the canoe, or ride the air around my head, but after I've paddled awhile they disappear. Of everything else in the canoe, besides me, the mosquitoes like the strip of Velcro along *Loon*'s side the best. They walk fastidiously over it, one next to the wing of the other, probing, ever hopeful of a strike.

Thoreau is the only writer who can convey in the description of a mosquito or a common housefly a brief history of the western world. I don't know how he does it, but he can make a bug seem like Ulysses voyaging home after the battles of Troy.

At age twenty-seven, Henry David Thoreau moved a mile and a half from his family's home in Concord to begin his residence at Walden Pond. No man, or woman, has ever worked harder, or more diligently, at turning history, thoughts, walks, friends, and neighbors into literature; nor over a longer period of time. It's no accident that his name is a worldwide beacon for anyone who cares about the natural world. Thoreau invented himself for that purpose.

Times have changed. The whole Northeast has changed. His pond has changed. The Thoreau family pencil factory has gone out of business. Most of us bear scant resemblance in looks, or habits, to the qualities Thoreau prized, but then who does measure up? What hasn't changed is what he put down in his journals about nature and human nature. His papers and personal effects have been passed down for generations as heirlooms through different members of the family. Some have become part of the larger treasure troves of important institutions, particularly the Morgan Library in New York, which possesses a supply of original pencils from the Thoreau pencil factory. They not only own the original journals but also the pine box Thoreau built to house and carry them.

I knew Willard Trask, a translator of Inuit songs and oral tales, during his last years in New York. He suffered from terrible emphysema. At the end of his life, he lived a horizontal existence because the energy required to move up and down stairs caused him much pain. On my occasional trips to New York, I used to visit and listen to him talk about the North and tell stories of his youth in Paris during the roaring twenties. Once, in passing, he mentioned his fascination with the box Thoreau had built to house his journals. He said he wasn't even sure if it existed, but he'd love to see it, if it did. I had never heard of it, but I did work for the Library of the Boston Athenaeum where a little digging revealed that the journals and the box were in New York at the Morgan Library not a mile from where Willard lived.

I secured us permission to see the box. The Athenaeum was a sister institution to the Morgan. The day we went, Willard was thrilled. However, my letter of introduction, and its request, were received coolly. We were given no more than a supervised viewing of journal material brought to us by an aloof white-gloved assistant librarian.

We said, "We didn't mean the journals. We want to see the box." The young man seemed at a loss. He retreated, twiddling his gloved fingers and shaking his head. He conferred with another librarian, who motioned over a third librarian, who went off to further confer with a fourth, older woman librarian, who shook her head. Whereupon the aloof assistant librarian showed the others my letter of introduction. They talked quietly together.

Willard leaned toward me and said, "What do you think it's called when three or more librarians confer?"

I said I didn't know. Before Willard could tell me, the young man in the white gloves approached to say, "Normally visitors are not allowed in our closed stacks, but follow me, please."

Down we went, curling around one of those snail-shell–shaped metal staircases, deep into the maw of the library. Willard became excited when we actually spied the box sitting on its metal shelf. We were not allowed to touch it. The librarian opened it and turned it around for us, his white-gloved hands like those of a magician about to demonstrate a trick.

The box was magic enough. The side facing us opened out and down, when a small brass hook was undone, to reveal each journal's spine, starting at the far left with the first year, moving to the last year's journal at the far right. It must have been easy for Thoreau to choose the journal he wished to work on; to slide it out and slip it back in when he finished. This drop-door feature, along with the handle on the top of the box, transforms this plain pine box, resembling a carpenter's toolbox, into a portable bookshelf. Willard finished feasting his eyes and we left, thanking the librarian profusely. The young man's quizzical look made me realize he didn't understand what Willard and I perceived in the box. Even now I wonder what fascinated Willard about the box. I never had the chance to ask him. The climb down and the climb back up the spiral staircase aggravated his emphysema and made reaching the comfort of his apartment all he was capable of that day.

Months passed before I could return to New York. In the meantime, Willard died, carrying with him his fascination for Thoreau's box and the answer to what three or more librarians are called when they confer. For my part, the box's simple construction, the few screws, the unpretentious pine wood, and its rubbed, carried, dinged, and knocked-about appearance made it seem lonesome among the pristine volumes and the protective, white-gloved librarians of the Morgan.

Throeau is lucky his box, and the journals it holds, are in such caring hands. Librarians too are deep dreamers.

By the afternoon the little insect demons are bouncing lazily against the tent. The heat has not only gotten to them; I am baked. On a clear July day, if there's no wind, any tent becomes an oven. I gird myself with a small black headnet and plenty of bug dope before I dismantle the tent, roll my pack, and steady the canoe while I load. I push off into the river around five.

Sore as I am, paddling feels good. My strokes and the current carry me into a new part of the river. The rock-strewn shores are disappearing; first the riverbanks are sandier, then they change back to green and rocks. I paddle through a borderland between a hard, bony geology and a softer, more pliable one. On the map I see ahead one of those small, black Rs indicating rapids. I won't know until I get there how severe they are, or how long they run.

As I come to the bend, the telltale rumble greets me. I stop. Out of the sand grows the dusty green-leafed flower with the pink bloom, river beauty, or, more formally, *Epilobium latifolium*. It grows in abundance here and is edible. It tastes like spinach. The blend of sand's flesh tone with the light-green, almost white-green leaves of the river beauty, capped by the dazzle of each pink bloom outstrips any composition of Georgia O'Keeffe's, especially when I'm down on my hands and knees with my eyes only inches from the blossom. It's a hardy flower in every respect: I've seen it blooming happily under two inches of water after the river's sudden rise. It doesn't care. It can wait for the water to recede.

I brew tea thinking about Back and his senior officer, Franklin, two men who knew little about sustaining themselves on the land. Compared to the Inuit, none of us does. Back's small expedition with ten men was successful. They carried most of their food. Everyone survived and although they mapped little new coastline, they discovered an inland route to the Arctic Ocean. Their main diet was pemmican, a mixture of sun-dried, pounded buffalo, moose, or caribou meat, packed in ninety-pound hide containers with melted tallow poured over it. "Quality" pemmican had berries mixed in.

Ten years later, in 1845, Sir John Franklin's last undertaking created one of the British navy's greatest disasters. Command of the expedition should have gone to a younger man, but the Admiralty felt they had enough information to solve the riddle of the Northwest Passage and gave the command to the sixty-year-old Franklin, as a tribute to his life's achievements in the

Arctic. With 129 men and two ships, the *Erebus* and the *Terror*, Franklin set sail from England. They never returned.

Not until Robert Scott died in Antarctica did England have as great a tragic hero as Franklin. No fewer than seventy-two expeditions were mounted, many sponsored by Lady Franklin, to determine the fate of her husband and his men. No complete written record has been found, but their sad story has been pieced together.

After living on their ships, stuck in the ice for two years off the northwest coast of King William Island, less than halfway to their goal, the men abandoned the *Erebus* and the *Terror*. The remaining 105 men, minus their commander, who had died in 1847, began walking south along the west shore of King William Island. As the island lay due north of the Back River, they hoped to cross the short span of open water and travel inland until they reached help. None made it. Along with human error, severe conditions, and plain bad luck, their lack of knowledge about the land and its natives contributed to their death.

One incident, told by a family of Inuit to one of the search parties, related how the family had found a small group of men on the ice. The men did not look well and the Inuit were scared to stay with them. It was difficult enough to provide for their own families, let alone a group of starving white men. The Inuit hunters killed several seals and left them on the ice for the whites. Days later, after the white men had left, the Inuit returned and were amazed to find the entrails not eaten. To them, the guts were the most nutritious part, and absolutely necessary for survival.

Everything here has to adapt to the vagaries of the Arctic, the severity of its conditions; even modern man, who imports what he needs to create a home. I have a friend who says I "spend" my way rather than "earn" my way down rivers. By this I take it he means the amount of food I carry, plus the ultra-modern equipment, reflect an inflated idea of the comfort level I require.

Damn right. But can you go back? I certainly could trim down, but return to the old ways? The Inuit don't go back, the Indians don't go back, white people wouldn't know how. And how far back should one go? I haven't heard of anyone who hasn't embraced some piece of the modern world to ease the time-consuming business of survival.

The rapid turns out to have one tight spot. As a rule, I try to land, scout, and shoot a rapid on the river's inside curve, if there is an inside curve. There the water is usually quieter. I've never had the courage to follow a route guessed at across from the riverbank I stand on. Here one large rock breaks the surface, pushing two billowing white wings of wave around either side. The wave I'll have to miss sweeps to within several feet of shore. I want to sneak by the wave's tail without encountering its vertical thrust. At the same time, I must avoid hitting any of the large boulders that have fallen into the river: in between them, contradictory waves collide. Their effect on a canoe would be like being in a plane when it flies into bad air, or driving on a highway when gusts of wind buffet the car.

I have already cracked one paddle blade while dragging it across rocks to slow *Loon* down. I carry three paddles, and need two to take the canoe's weight off my neck as I portage. When I get back to where I've beached her at the head of the rapid, I make a point of telling *Loon* what we want to do. I worry that while I study a rapid, *Loon* will drift around the corner heading toward disaster. If I'm not going to shoot a rapid, I carry a load down with me. Sometimes I do anyway. If we don't shoot the rough water, I've already portaged one load. If the rapid is a rough one, taking a load over as I scout the water at least lightens *Loon*. Then, too, I can use my distinctive blue pack to mark an aspect of the rapid I need to be wary about. Because I hadn't bothered to take one with me, I carry a pack back to mark the large rock and prop it up—a silent judge of how we'll do. I put the spray skirt on and off we go.

I used to shoot rapids at a full gallop, figuring speed to be an ally. I don't anymore. There are bursts of speed, but the best moments come when the water works for me, sucking me into a V, nursing the bow between rocks, or providing an added nudge. Then, the water's rebound off a rock buffers *Loon* from hitting it and, at the rapid's end, spits me out like a watermelon seed. Those are the best moments.

The last section of the rapid is a tumble of rocks—even the water has to feel its way through here. In sloppy water I pull out and portage the forty yards to the calm water on the other side. In the sand are tracks of a big wolf. Wolves often follow the course of the river in search of food.

Beyond a pebble island, under a hot sun, I camp on flat ground in late afternoon. Sandy patches show through the thin grass skin. This could pass for a lawn, or a golf course. It's the floor of a valley lying between two steep eskers that shoot up three and four hundred feet. The small river responsible for carving the valley runs quietly through a corner of it, dwarfed by its creation.

The river's ground rules change. Here sand softens the color of the riverbanks and the land's contours. There is a greater variety of colored rocks along the shore. The ice and water mull over the river's trinkets and decide, as whimsically as a child would, what deserves a special spot.

Denny once said, "Thoreau's writing reminds me of the bits and pieces you'd find in a nine-year-old boy's pocket."

Across from me is a steep pile of boulders pushed up with massive force. Common sense dictates that the largest stones should be on the bottom, but they're not. It's a principle of physics that the larger objects in a pile rise when pushed or shaken. I've done it at home shaking the bowl of change on my bureau. The quarters rise to the top.

The rest of the evening features dustings of rain and gray clouds with ragged patches of blue. The color has a delicate quality, smooth and soft as a baby's tongue. I go to bed thinking about Denny and Thoreau—and the land that shaped them.

People have squeezed our woods, meadows, and open spaces into a marginal existence. The erosion of what Thoreau meticulously cataloged continues. The remaining open areas have been hard fought for and expensive to keep from the developer. The spirit to conserve and reform hasn't died, but it's hard to tell who's winning. Though the intentions were good, one casualty is Thoreau's Walden Pond. I joined Denny there last spring toward the end of an unusual canoe trip he had undertaken: paddling from west to east across Massachusetts. Because the rivers in the state flow north to south, his trip involved crossing four watershed divides and fourteen different rivers. Half of them he paddled upstream. He hoped to speak up for our need to protect clean water where it still exists and to clean the water up where it is polluted. He believes that if individuals don't assume personal responsibility for the earth's resources close to home, there won't be any left. Denny set out to capture media attention, hoping to raise people's awareness. He did. Local news stations across the state ran clips on his progress. During the month of his paddle numerous papers, among them *The Boston Globe* and *The New York Times*, ran articles on his "Paddle for Clean Water." Denny asked school children to sign his canoe as a petition that he would deliver to a very un-environmentally-minded governor.

The day he finished his trip, forty canoes paddled with him down the Charles River. Several hundred people walked behind him as he portaged his petition canoe from the river up Beacon Hill to the State House. A police cruiser led the way, and traffic stopped. The governor was not present, but several politicians, environmentalists, and Denny spoke.

The day I joined him at Walden Pond, a clear day in mid-April, I found him tucked away at the far end of the pond working with a television news crew. When they finished, Denny paddled in to meet me. We drifted near the center of the pond. He picked up his cellular phone. "Thoreau, Emerson, and Channing used the pulpit, the newspaper, the lecture, the pamphlet, the book, and the letter to convey their ideas and feelings," Denny said. "Nowadays we have radio, television, and mobile phones. I can as easily sit in my canoe and make calls about clean water as another person can sit in his BMW and make business deals."

"What do you tell them?" I asked.

"That I'm an individual who has paddled the last twenty-seven days across the state of Massachusetts to bring attention to an issue as relevant here as it is in California: clean water."

"Let's call California," I said.

Denny had the numbers of several California radio talk shows. We put through some calls, but as spontaneous as radio shows sound, they're highly programmed. They did not wish to talk to a guy in a canoe, floating around on Walden Pond. They said to call back next week.

We drifted some more.

"The White House," Denny said, and dialed the number. The first person to answer passed him on until he reached a high-ranking aide on the Reagan staff who expressed interest. Denny explained what he had done, why he had done it, and where he was calling from: "A canoe," he said, motioning me to splash some water. "I'm at Walden Pond, the historical focal point of nature's conscience."

"Walden who?" the woman asked.

"Walden Pond, where Thoreau lived and wrote his classic book called *Walden*," Denny explained.

She didn't get it, but she thanked Denny for his support of the President and hung up. We laughed as we paddled in to shore.

On shore stood the Walden Pond ranger-guide assigned to Denny. We were still laughing over the phone conversation with the woman at the White House.

"At least the pond is still here," I said to Denny reassuringly.

"Yes, the pond's still here," the ranger who had overheard me allowed, "but don't drink the water." I noticed a two-abreast walkway near completion ringing the pond.

The ranger-guide, wearing khaki and Robin Hood green, saw my astonishment.

"Too many people tramping around the pond have caused severe erosion," he said. "The new walkway will preserve the integrity of the hillsides and allow more people—mothers with baby carriages and people in wheelchairs—to enjoy the solitude of the pond."

"How many people visit the pond?" Denny asked.

"Roughly 500,000 a year," said the ranger-guide. "Mostly spring through fall. We've cut down on the available parking to limit the number of visitors. Now only 200,000 come, but it never ends. We've got to fight a proposed development next door as well as get the school across the highway to limit access to their parking lot."

The man was clearly uncomfortable with the pond's state of affairs. As his face contorted in his effort to make peace with his conflicts, he said, "Ours is an age of compromise."

"I guess the walkway is kind of like girdling the bark off a tree to protect it from the ravages of porcupines," Denny ventured.

The ranger-guide agreed a little too enthusiastically as if he believed girdling to be something good for the tree.

As Denny pulled the canoe out, planning to portage it over the walkway, over the railroad tracks, and through the woods to the Sudbury River, I couldn't help thinking about the new walkway. It may benefit the people who come to use it, and the management policy of the pond, but not the pond itself. There was no benefit to the pond. The ranger-guide was right: we live in an age of compromise, violent compromise. Ever since the idea of compromise was embraced, every power under the sun has been used to ensure that the rights of people are protected and the rights of every other creature are compromised. As much as the walkway will provide full access for all, it creates a cage, or glass case, around the pond; a good viewing area. When the walkway is complete, the pond will be like a natural zoo.

Denny must have been thinking similar thoughts. As he hoisted the canoe up on his shoulders, crossed the highway, and headed toward the railroad tracks and the woods beyond, he yelled to me.

"Walden who? Thoreau what?"

The following morning, after breakfast, I stand with my back to the river saying good-bye to this esker valley. The high green banks, the walled-in feeling, and the quiet of a new day make me feel comfortable here, as if the valley were a gigantic nest and *Loon* and I had been its eggs for the night. Standing in this quiet place, I feel a pull inside me I haven't felt before. I am overtaken by an image of my turning into a piece of the land, a carpet of grass, a rock, the hair on my body becoming alders, my shape part of the land's contour. Over the edge of the tall esker, hundreds of feet up, glides a powerful-looking bird. Riding the updrafts, it wheels slowly out over the valley. I can't tell what type of raptor it is. I see big pronounced Vs at the wing tips. As gracefully as it came, with only the slightest tilt of wing, the bird slides back over the esker's rim out of sight. I turn and pack up.

On the river I place the thought of the bird aside, and the shiver of excitement I felt watching it. I come to a set of three rapids and begin negotiating them. After the first rapid, the river inhales and circles into a deep bay. The banks are hundreds of feet high. Along their top I see a hairline of green slumping over the edge. The erosion up there is not in the river's domain, but is the work of ground squirrels, rain, and wind.

Being in no hurry to shoot another rapid, I drift into the

bay. Above me where the cliff face turns the corner downstream, near the top, the same large bird rises up. It flies directly off. I feel as if I've seen an echo. Had I heard chirping, or did I only imagine it coupled with my immediate thought that this might be where its nest is? At the opposite end of the bay, I beach *Loon* and walk to the lowest edge of the cliff to look for it. Even there I have to scramble a sharp zigzag course uphill. Once I'm on top the walking is smooth. The view is forever. To be this high up in the tundra is like flying. *Loon* appears as a tiny white dot. I lie down. I peer cautiously over the edge at two places, but don't see a nest. I feel like giving up but look over the edge a last time. There's the outcrop of clay with claw marks, and even a feather. I see the nest. Only the outer crescent of tangled sticks is visible, the rest lies buried under several feet of clay, topsoil, and tufts of green grass. Were the chicks buried under there? The eggs? How lonely the large bird seems to me now. Instead of the thrill I had hoped for, a cold shiver runs over my body. To be buried under an earthslide seems a cruel death. Does the bird I saw return here to mourn? My own memories of the birds hitting the windows get tangled up in the twigs and sticks below me. I climb down to get the feather. It's from a rough-legged hawk.

Back at *Loon* I'm thoughtful, moody. I paddle out to the start of the next rapid and look up to say good-bye . . . to something, but I don't know what.

There are certain don'ts involved in shooting rapids. One is don't shoot rapids into early-morning sun. The glare off the water hides rocks, dazzles the eyes, and puts you in danger. The rapid in front of me has the low angle of the morning sun on it. I could wait a few hours. I could portage. But something reckless in me pushes me to shoot it. The sun turns the water to gold, the rocks to black, and sketches the drift of the current and outlines the eddies. I run it, a rapid transformed into sunlight. At the bottom I promise *Loon* I won't make a habit of it.

I rediscover a paddling rhythm late in the day. I like to paddle; the sheer pleasure of it pulls me forward. My next major landmark will be the Baillie River, which enters the Back from the right, or south.

I let go of my vigilance and my mind opens. As my body works and the scene expands, I'm drawn into a reverie. Leave it to the French to untangle such a subtle thing from "dream" and "daydream" and call it reverie. Nighttime dreams are masculine; they can get pushy. They can be violent. A daydream seems closer to reverie, but not as deep—it glides over the surface of things, a lacquer finish, bright but with little substance. A reverie is feminine, but not without the capacity to startle.

In my reverie I see a photograph my brother owns, a late-nineteenth-century photograph of a man sitting in a workroom, a private place of his own, a nest. Wood-carving tools and ship models lie about him. He holds one model in his lap on a leather apron. His beard is as white as his shirt. Light comes through a half-open door on the left, shining off his apron and the covering of his small, portable workbench. His ankles and legs look swollen from failing circulation. Many Victorian photographs are formal. This is not. The old man—my great-great-grandfather—is neither dressed formally nor seems ill at ease. It's as if, during the time it took to take the photograph, he ignored the admonition to sit up and smile and instead relaxed and sank into—into what?

I know this about him. From the age of thirteen, when he first went to sea, ships were his life. From cabin boy on a relative's clipper ship in the China trade, he became mate, then captain, then owner of his own clipper ships. He built up and lost three separate fortunes. He saw steam replace sail. I wonder if, by the time of the photograph, he felt he'd become a ghost in his own time.

I see a man in his reverie, remembering a lifetime of voyages. The clipper ship models he builds, are they toys? I doubt it. As he carves, his hands move by reflex with a will of their own. They hold up their work to his eye for adjustment. Isn't he dreaming? Doesn't he hear the sigh and creak of rigging in his workroom? Doesn't he taste the salt, see the flying fish in the South China Sea, smell the tarred lines? The ship models around him are the tangible bits, the merest hints of his younger self, confident, sure, and quick. They are his reverie.

The river widens. The wind starts to rise from the southeast. I have a half-mile slog into it to get *Loon* under the lee of a thirty-foot clay bank. It could have been the maquette for the morning's larger cliffs. The river constantly licks at its bottom. Like sharks attacking a wounded whale, I imagine the icebergs scraping, gouging, and tearing out chunks of bank in spring runoff. The uncovered strata of different-color soils, compressed over thousands of years, create a horizontal marbling. Cross-sections of old ground squirrel colonies are visible near the top. A layer of moss and grass rooted in the tundra's thin topsoil slumps like a

badly fitted toupee over the bank's brow. As I look up from my seat, my eye is jolted by the edge where this green line meets the China blue sky. In their need to reach the river, occasional streams have eaten through the bank, creating gullies leading inland. At the foot lies a narrow strip of beach. The water close to it is brown from the current's constant laving. Paddling close to the beach through the silty water, I see flecks of silver, the quick sides of minnows glinting in the sun as they scatter from *Loon*'s shadow. The perspective line of the bank diminishes ahead. I have a long paddle.

I settle in, switching sides frequently hoping that will lessen the ache in my fingers and back. I find a rhythm to suit the length of the day when out of a draw trots a large white wolf. There is no way for me to be perfectly still, but I try. For a marvelous fifty feet, I see the wolf first. It's a male, old and favoring his left front paw. He comes down the beach. I sit still, watching. He sees me but doesn't bolt. We each look at the draw. Looking back at each other, we realize we can both arrive at the draw at the same time. Because of his foot, he'd rather not scale the bank, but he can't stay where he is. In a split second the wolf mounts the bank in diagonal bounds and vanishes, but for a moment, we bridged a gap and shared a thought through our eyes. Neither of us reacted out of fear. By comparison, the next several days hold nothing as exciting. They are tame, but not uneventful.

Each day a startling white-gold sun, like some strange potentate from the East, climbs into the sky. I feel the full weight of it. More and more I see the fruits of its labor; the air feels thick with the fecundity of the land. I see families of geese, mother caribou, and their calves. Once in the evening, over the course of paddling half a mile, I count eleven different ptarmigan broods. Like a pack of struck marbles, the chicks scatter for cover at their mother's warning call. Small winged life arrives in profusion: black flies, mosquitoes, horseflies, and bumblebees. Each butterfly brings me to a halt while my eyes dance after it. The sky seems one pulse of wings, with more life in it than the ground. The water's surface remains in constant motion, alive with swirls, rings, and jumping fish. I see fresh wolf tracks in the moist sand, and running parallel to them the unmistakable prints of a bear. Under this sun they appear to have formed an unlikely alliance.

The main channel becomes tough to follow because of the sand. If I lose the main channel there's barely a paddle-blade of water. I coast and push through the shallows. By careful reading of the ribbed sand passing underneath us, I navigate back to the main channel. The wave patterns made by the sand tell me the current's direction. I want to traverse the patterns.

A herd of muskox grazes, their woolly bodies dark moving spots in the tundra plain. Of the thirty I count, ten are babies. In the foreground is a flock of mixed Canadas and stark-white snow geese. The longer I look, the more I see. The more I see, the more I look, until the scene becomes a fluid meshing of animal, insect, and bird life. From the tiniest fleck of soil to the largest muskox, everything in front of me has its place in the whole. I stay all afternoon on the periphery of their circle, under the weight of that terrific heat, until in one brief moment something in me, some ice-blue fist, thaws. The circle expands around me. The elements that make me up have been reordered, like a fraction turned into a whole number. Concern about my dad and Una fades. The animals and land in front of me now seem brighter, clearer.

As evening comes on, I camp nearby and happen to look up as a blinding red-gold sun moves serenely from under a purple cloud.

That night I think of another man I met during my hectic fund-raising, Edmund Carpenter. I was told by a friend of his that he might be interested in my trip. He was a filmmaker and ethnologist who had traveled widely and spent many years in the

Arctic on St. Lawrence Island. Now in his seventies, he lived in New York.

I called to make an appointment. A voice answering said, "Yes?"

I asked if I could speak with Mr. Carpenter.

"Yes."

I waited, said who I was, and why I was calling.

"Yes."

I mentioned the name of Mr. Carpenter's friend who recommended I call.

"That's fine."

Finally realizing I was speaking to Mr. Carpenter, I asked if I could come for a short visit.

"Yes," he said.

I asked which morning or afternoon of such and such days would be better for him.

"Any one is fine, just come ahead."

I found this a peculiar response for a wealthy New Yorker. I decided he must be extremely bored or eccentric.

I stepped out of the elevator into a room with a vaulted ceiling, painted cloud white, onto gleaming hardwood floors. Full-blown trees grew in the room's corners. The expanse of glass that covered the north wall looked out onto Central Park. There was no street noise. I wouldn't have known I was in New York. In the center of the floor was the room's only piece of furniture, a large wooden desk covered with mountains of paper. Behind it sat Mr. Carpenter, who rose to greet me. After a brief conversation, he invited me to join him for lunch. We took the elevator one flight up.

Upstairs I found more of everything: trees, space, glass, view. On the walls hung pieces of the world's cultural past, from a large Max Ernst painting to what attracted me the most, a fragment of an ancient Peruvian screen made with bright-yellow parrot feathers.

During our meal he was gracious in every way.

We returned downstairs so he could show me his collection of Inuit artifacts. Afterward we passed back through the large room where he and his assistants work. I could hear the scholarly shuffle of papers, the scurry of feet.

Halfway across the floor, Mr. Carpenter said, "As I am currently fully committed, I cannot help you financially. But I would like to hear from you in the fall. Seventy-two days alone is an awfully long time." Then he continued as if he had been mulling over this thought and was speaking his mind out loud:

". . . and this is Mr. Perkins who is going for seventy-two days by himself in the Arctic. When he returns, he is going to write a classic!" He spoke this in a loud voice, bearing down sarcastically on the word "classic."

The room became quiet. I wished I could evaporate. We arrived at the elevator door in silence.

"Travel safely," he said sincerely. "Good-bye."

Of all the gifts I received, of all the survival equipment I've brought with me, his remark is one I value. It's lightweight, takes up no space, and doesn't get spent. Every time I think of it, it helps keep me from getting a swelled head. How many times since I started have I heard Mr. Carpenter's words echo in the river, the sky, the rocks, the mosquitoes' drone:

". . . and this is Mr. Perkins, who is going to the Arctic . . ."

The good weather lasts until morning. The next day is as indifferent as my disposition. The sky is an unpleasant gray and the sun has not troubled to come out. I pack up and paddle, wanting to reach Hawk Rapids. By noon the sky darkens and there is a hot sluggishness in the air. The storm gathers throughout the afternoon with a silent, ominous intensity, like a mob assembling. I pitch my tent well in advance of its arrival and secure *Loon* with several heavy rocks. Then I go for a walk.

As if a reprieve has been granted, the sky suddenly shatters

into chunks of cloud that seem as reluctant to leave their place as the wind is insistent on their moving. Around their lighter edges come and go shafts of biblical sunlight.

I walk for no reason. I've been lucky with weather so far, but there's an edginess in me today I can't shake. Like the gathering storm, I can't seem to make up my mind whether to sit still or jump right up and scream. To be out of the wind's force, I hunker down behind a rock. One of those rays of sunlight appears on my right sleeve. Quickly my left hand jumps to cup it, only to have it appear on the back of my hand. As a child, I spent hours sitting at our dining-room table lost in this cat-and-mouse game. As I play now, among the rocks, a sadness I hadn't asked for arrives. The playfulness is gone. The game's futility glares at me, like a small angry animal annoyed at my attempts to clutch it.

After leaving Ireland I leaped the major hurdle set up by Una's mother: a nine-to-five job with a future. The year before I had begun talking with an insurance brokerage firm about parlaying my art background into a service for their clients who owned valuable collections. Insurance people rarely have the interest, the capacity, or the time to properly handle the objects collected by individuals and companies. I proposed to assist their brokers with this business. The firm was large enough to experiment with the concept of a Fine Art Council and it offered me the opportunity to prove it worked. I assumed I would live in Boston, occasionally visiting the corporate headquarters in New York. When The Company approved my position, I was called by my new boss, Dave, who said, "Congratulations. You start in New York June first. We'll move you in May."

When I called, Una was thrilled for me, but she had her doubts about New York. So did I, but in my excitement, I overlooked them. I was about to learn the meaning of an old Celtic saying, "You don't know your mistake until you make it."

Una came to the States and we flew into LaGuardia from Boston at night, passing low over the tip of the island. The multitude of light clusters and strings seemed like the ribbons tied around a package. Our doubts dwindled in the excitement. We felt a heady tug as if pulled into a huge dream, New York's dream, a river of dreams that pours constantly into the city. That night, the city seemed like poetry in the way it compressed all life, all races, all feelings into a small island and then added music.

Everything was new: my job, our being together, our apartment. From the front windows of our fourth-floor walk-up in Brooklyn Heights, we looked across the East River to a strange forest of skyscrapers into which I reluctantly disappeared each day—often for ten to twelve hours at a time. In one fell swoop respectability had been bestowed on me. I was sharing my life with the woman I loved. I was dealing with valuable art, helping people unravel, prevent, and understand the problems that owning possessions entailed.

We had been in New York for two weeks. My first work morning, I slipped out of bed, put on a suit, and came back to watch Una sleep. She was barely visible among the pillows and covers except for a tangle of fair hair. Without thinking I woke her to say good-bye. Jokingly I asked, "What about breakfast?" She got up, cooked me something, and left me to eat it alone. The night before she had said to me, "I don't even have a garden." This wouldn't be easy for her.

A woman, whose Park Avenue penthouse was full of art, asked The Company up for an interview. Dave brought me along in case there were art-related insurance problems. We sat in her living room, surrounded by beautiful things. The couch and chairs were an off white, the rug pure white. Above the dark wood paneling of the mantel hung the culprit: a not-so-large Degas pastel of a woman bather. After she recently redecorated the living room at vast expense, her insurance broker informed her that the value of the pastel had risen to over one million dollars and it had to be wired directly to an alarm system or insurance wouldn't cover it. She refused to disrupt her new living room to accommodate the insurance company; she felt the company should accommodate her.

"If you can help me," she said, "you have my business."

After I outlined how it could be done, Dave talked about the total review of their insurance. Out of the corner of my eye, I saw a small, lonely shape set out on a long march across the white rug toward the woman's feet. It was a cockroach. I considered my options while Dave talked. I could ignore it; I could stand up and grind it into the spotless white rug; I could pick it up . . . but do what with it? I decided to consider it a relative of Don Marquis's cockroach, Archy, in his book *The Lives and Times of Archy and Mehitabel*, when Dave, without breaking his sentence, stood up, pulled out his breast pocket handkerchief, scooped Archy's relative off the rug, and stuffed the handkerchief back in his breast pocket. The woman of the house seemed not to notice. Our interview ended, and we left.

Within a day Dave told me we had won the account. The broker upstairs, who worked with the husband's corporation, wondered what we had done to impress the wife so favorably. "Whatever it was," he said to Dave, "send that guy to solve her art problem."

Within a week her Degas dilemma was solved. Thanks to the wizardry of modern technology, a transistor alarm chip had been inconspicuously attached to the back of the frame. An underwriter from the insurance company stood beside us admiring the pastel over the mantel, now connected, but not wired, to the alarm system. It occurred to me to ask what covered the pastel: glass or Plexiglas?

"Why, Plexiglas, of course," the woman said.

Of all I had accomplished, I had totally missed the major threat to this work of art. I suggested we take the bather off the wall, and explained the danger.

"If you or your maid pass a dust cloth over the surface of the Plexiglas in order to clean it, you'll create an electrical charge on the Plexiglas. Even if this is done only a few times, as much as a third of the pastel could pull off the paper and stick to the back of the Plexiglas. This would be a very expensive mistake."

She agreed. Between my boss, the cockroach, and me, we had won a friend for life. Not every account had as happy an outcome, but I was learning, or soon would learn, to take the bad with the good.

¤ ¤ ¤

One evening, as I arrived home late, Una met me at the door. She was excited about a woman she met who was giving away kittens.

"Could we get one? Actually two, so the one would have the company of the other?" she asked. "You'd like a kitty, wouldn't you? Let's at least go see."

We went to the address. A middle-aged woman with a low, sweet voice came down to let us in, whispering not to mention "cats" on the stairs. The landlord had told her to get rid of them. She ushered us in and quickly locked the door. Looking around, I quietly counted while she took Una to one of the cages. There were seventy-seven cats stacked from floor to ceiling in wire cages in this tiny one-room apartment. Others lay curled on the bed in the middle of the room or roamed delicately on the thin wire across cage tops. Live roaches swarmed over everything. Killing them seemed the sole sad amusement of the caged cats.

The woman said, "I have eighty-seven cats. Strays mostly. Runaways. There's a network of us in New York that save cats from the streets. Now, here is a litter of four left on someone's front yard." In this litter, Una saw a particularly shy gray kitten. She called me over. The gray one she liked was too scared to be held. We chose a companion for it, a year-old tiger cat, thanked the woman—who was only too glad to see us take them—and left.

The woman loved cats, that was clear, but to love them she had to keep them in cages. If I were a cat, I might prefer the street to life in a cage.

Back in our apartment, Una put the gray kitten down and with a scrabble of tiny claws it disappeared down the hall, under the bed. Una named her Gray Cat, but I began calling her the Lobster, because all I saw when I stooped to say hello were her two yellow eyes looking out at me from under the bed. Una spent her free time with the two cats and they became her friends. As I was away working, they showed as much interest in me as they would in a cold wind. If I had taken the time to notice, I might have seen Una was more and more adrift. I might have seen her mind leave the table at dinner and go elsewhere.

In a world of machines and human pressure, the body begins to hum and sing and whistle until it either adjusts or snaps. I didn't fully appreciate the double-edged quality of my home life, or of my supervisor's constant remark, "It's only a matter of time." I often repeated it to myself as encouragement, thinking he meant "before it all works out."

At dinner one night, Una told me she was going home to Ireland to pick up a few things. What she didn't tell me was that she wasn't coming back.

The day she left the apartment, I put her one suitcase in the cab, held the door while she got in, and told the driver the airline she was booked on. Had she looked back Una would have seen me waving with the larger cat in my arms and, pressed against the apartment window upstairs, a small gray face looking out.

With Una away, I redoubled my efforts at work. Things were going well. I began to feel more at ease and sought out the tiny, unremarked natural aspects of the city that contradicted all the steel and concrete. I tried to spend some of each day observing something alive other than people, pigeons, and gulls. One lunch hour, eating an orange at the corner of Wall and Water streets, I discovered a hidden ornithological subculture unanticipated by the city planners. In the streetlight above me a horizontal pipe served as part of the light's supporting armature. In the small orifice of the pipe, two house sparrows had made their nest. Traveling around the city, it didn't take long to confirm that each corner's traffic light doubled as a safe nesting site for sparrows.

I look up from my thoughts and out at the river. I don't know how long I've been sitting braced against the rock. I see the wind is strong from the white caps on the water. Shafts of light still play at the edges of the dark clouds. The air feels heavy, like rain. My knees are sore. I stretch.

I wasn't alone in applying observational skills at work. One of the firm's partners, the chief counsel, heard that several of our department's suggestions had gained currency with upper management and that I had some responsibility for this. He called me up to his office to have a look at me.

Mr. Groton was a small man with oiled dark hair, glasses, and a nervous habit of touching his thumb to the fingers on his left hand while he talked. His small fingernails were immaculate. The roundness of his glasses frames mirrored the miniature moon shape of his pale face. His office was hung with reproductions of Persian miniatures. His sofa was the color of tomato soup. The magnificent black-and-white photographs of mountains behind his desk prompted me to ask if he climbed.

"No," he said. "I just like to go and look." Much the way he was looking at me, I thought. The mountain photographs seemed an incongruous part of the office until I realized how perfectly suited they were to everything else: reduced to a manageable size. He welcomed me to the "family" and stressed, more than once, the importance of the firm's chain of command, and the virtue of patience.

Riding down in the elevator to the seventh floor where I worked, I recalled another insurance lawyer I knew through the poems he had written. His name was Wallace Stevens. Unlike Mr. Groton, he lived in an ever-expanding world. Reading a poem of his, I marvel at his ability to turn words into wonder and wonder into words. Times were different in the forties and fifties. Stevens lived in a house a ten-minute walk from his office in Hartford. I'm told he composed many of his best poems during that walk to work, or on a walk during lunch. One of his indulgences was to have fresh roses on his desk in a silver bowl.

Arriving for work, or returning from lunch, he would call to his secretary and say, "Miss Niff, take a poem."

As weeks passed into months, I grew sadder. The difference between what I'd hoped to do and what I was actually doing became increasingly clear.

I worked for a company occupying fourteen floors of a building at the heel of Wall Street. Twelve hundred people worked on these floors and formed the nucleus for a larger, worldwide organization numbering in the thousands. I worked in a cubicle next to the next cubicle, part of each floor's honeycomb of cubicles. The floor below ours had recently been modernized—to make the cubicles the same dark gray. Now the men and women in their dark suits seemed to detach themselves from the fabric of their cubicles to walk around. Upstairs I had a brown desk and a blue chair on missing rollers. I had a push-button phone, a Rolodex file, memo pads with the Company name and my name printed on them, and a secretary who also worked for five other men. (I gained a great respect for the women in The Company, for what they had to put up with from men.) I wasn't within twenty feet of a window, but I could see out one. The view was another building, like ours, except its windows were reflective glass. In them I could see the East River, and FDR Drive in front of it. The water and sunlight were organized by the window squares, broken up in the wavy mirrored glass transforming each car, each straight line, and the water, into fun-house images. The windows turned inward at night, like a dirty sock turned inside out, to reveal other people working late in their honeycomb of cubicles.

I missed Una. I worried for us. Our phone calls became less frequent. Then all she couldn't bring herself to say arrived in a letter. She couldn't live in America, at least not in New York. She couldn't live where her feet couldn't touch the ground. She wished me luck. She hoped I would understand. What about me? I was left with a crushing job, an apartment, and two impossible cats. All of this, she said, was what I had wanted.

Within a week of Una's departure the cats turned wild. I never saw the shy kitten, and the other kept its distance. As I climbed the stairs each evening I would try to guess which part of the apartment they destroyed during the day.

I could return them to the cat woman, but that seemed cruel. I could find them another home, but who would take two wild cats? Humane societies keep cats for adoption, but kill them after a certain time. I decided to put them back on the street. At least they were spayed. On a Sunday, when fewer people would be out to notice, I took them across town. For a man who loved animals, I was betraying myself. But the two cats seemed elated looking into the overgrown vacant lot. *This* is the world we know, they seemed to say. Letting the cats go brought something to an end between Una and me, but I have never forgiven myself for abandoning the cats.

I dust off the back of my pants as I get up from behind the rock. The sunlight is gone. The river's color has grown darker. The wind is building. The clouds have bunched up again, dampening the intermittent sun to dull nickel before obscuring it completely. At their center the clouds are the color of a bruise. I start walking slowly back to the tent. I feel almost as numb as I did my last year in New York. Whenever I called home, my dad reminded me that I had a good job. He said there were plenty of girls, not that many good jobs. I was not sure I agreed with him, on either count.

A year after starting, I was upstairs with one of the partners discussing the potential for growth that fine art insurance could have for The Company. "Great," he said. "Put it in writing. Make an 'Action Plan.' Bring it to me. We'll start the ball rolling."

Business language is as exacting as any other, but it's not often exciting to read. I set out to write an exciting Action Plan.

By my elbow was *The Elements of Style* by Mr. Strunk and Mr. White. They suggested starting a composition of this nature with a quote or anecdote. I took to heart their plea for clear sentences, the power of metaphor, and *substance*. I chose an anecdote from *Alice in Wonderland*:

> "Cheshire Puss," she began, rather timidly . . . "Would you tell me, please, which way I ought to walk from here?"
>
> "That depends a good deal on where you want to get to," said the Cat.
>
> "I don't much care where—" said Alice.
>
> "Then it doesn't matter which way you walk," said the Cat.
>
> "—so long as I get *somewhere*," Alice added as an explanation.
>
> "Oh, you're sure to do that," said the Cat, "if you only walk long enough."

I went on to outline how, unlike Alice in the dark wood, The Company could travel quite far in this new area of business if they took several simple steps.

I went to deliver the first copy of my Action Plan to the partner who requested it. He was absent, but Mr. Groton stood in his doorway. He wore a dark-blue suit that showed his black hair to advantage and highlighted the pale color of his skin. He reminded me of a spider hovering at the edge of its web.

"What's that?" he asked, seeing the paper in my hand. I told him. He invited me into his office. "I would be glad to give it a read," he said. I thought this was generous of him.

He placed the paper on top of his briefcase and then said, "Tomorrow."

He offered me his hand. It felt warm and sticky.

I left to deliver the remaining copies of my Action Plan.

Tomorrow arrived and with it came a call from Mr. Groton. First, he said, he'd like us to have lunch. Then he changed his mind, and said, "No. What I have to say to you, I will tell you on the phone. You should not have written that Action Plan. I don't want you to circulate one copy of it, not even to the partner who asked you to write it. I think you've made a mistake." When I hung up, my boss, Dave, and my supervisor appeared at my desk: two heads, four arms, side by side. They were furious. They couldn't tell me in enough ways how upset they were that I had compared The Company to a *woman* and a *fairy tale*! Looking up at them, I saw Tweedledum and Tweedledee. I held my tongue.

As a rolled ball gradually loses momentum, my enthusiasm for The Company and its goals came to a stop. I walked the streets of the city, feeling the minotaur stalk me. To dodge him, I spent my time inside the smaller maze of The Company, in a warren of impossible relationships. At night New York had the unreal quality of an ocean liner that went nowhere, the lighted squares of apartment windows the berths on this immobile ship.

An uncle, who had worked in the city for twenty-three years, told me before I left Boston his conclusion about New York: "It feeds on its young."

One morning, on instinct, I went to the New York Public Library, the main branch on Fifth Avenue. I asked for a copy of *Narrative of the Arctic Land Expedition to the Mouth of the Great Fish River, 1833, 1834, and 1835* by George Back.

"I don't know. Let's see," the woman in front of me said. She tapped away at her console, waited, and then turned. "Yes. Here is your number, thirty-three. Just go to the Great South Hall and wait for the number to come up on the board."

I sat on a bench facing the board. Behind me I felt the presence of all those minds. I heard the sharp sound of a woman's high heels crossing the stone floor and a loud tuba noise as someone pushed back a chair. What brought me here?

When Back's journal arrived, I found a seat at a long table. In a black square sat a white 47 in front of me. I stared at the book, then at the number on the table. I hadn't seen the journal for nine years, not since I held it at the Boston Athenaeum. A voice in me said, "Look at it!"

I sensed something coming, the way you do in the air before a summer storm. Pressure was building inside my head. As dark as it seemed to be getting around me, I felt as bright and intense as a light bulb without a shade. "Focus on the book." I put my elbows on the table, put my head in my palms, and tried to block out the noise. It was all the books, wasn't it, that couldn't keep their mouths shut. I closed my eyes tight. I breathed in, but only inhaled the noise I was trying to keep out.

"I'm sorry, sir, but if you can't be quiet, you'll have to leave." A female voice broke through my thoughts. "You'll have to be quiet, or leave," she repeated. I looked up into the librarian's concerned face. I hadn't realized I'd made any noise, but scowling faces around the room showed me I had done something. My head felt light. Whatever had been going on in it vanished. I mumbled an apology and got up.

Pregnant with my own contradictions—my love of Una, my job, New York, the Arctic—I went slowly down the staircase, holding the brass banister. It felt cool. The lobby looked vast. I crossed the marble floor and walked outside. I didn't want to look behind me; like a slug I dragged a glittering slime of broken wishes.

Outside, I was surprised to see the sun. On the street, everything was hectic, crowded, and carrying on as normal. I still felt weak. I faltered at a white stone lion at the bottom of the stairs.

Just then a house sparrow landed behind the lion's right front paw holding a U-shaped crust of bread, larger than itself. It bit the crust in half, tore at it, then devoured it. The sparrow fought off the advances of other sparrows and a pigeon. I tried to watch the bird as it flew out of the sunlight into the shade across the street.

It was time to go: time to leave New York. As the fallen angel said, *Non serviam*. I saw that, as clearly as I saw the sparrow eat the crust. But what about my job?

I needn't have worried. Within a week of my resolve, they fired me. Nothing ceremonious. In his office, Mr. Groton told me that my job with The Company had ended. I could put my I.D. card on his desk, leave at five, and not come back. He said I would receive several months' severance pay. Not once did he look at me. He kept moving things around on his desk until he excused himself. If he had looked up, I would have thanked him. In the elevator going down to the seventh floor, my now ex-boss, Dave, shrugged.

"I'm sorry it did not work out. Your memo angered a lot of people, especially Mr. Groton."

I get back to camp as the storm breaks. I tumble inside the tent as the first large drops begin hammering. Sheets of rain wash across the landscape. The river's surface is alive, the rocks glisten. Small veins of rainwater twist their way through the stones and grass to the river. The puddles expose their bias toward the river when they overflow. Everything has a tilt. The three rocks squatting on *Loon*, equally spaced in a row, seem some odd triumvirate out enjoying the weather. A rumble of thunder rolls through half the sky, then a tremendous crash unleashes more rain. Every few minutes I'm surrounded by a white light, still and moving. I close my eyes. Rain becomes the sound in my head as most days it's the wind. I imagine it helps me slough off the skin of New York, my job, Una. In my mind, I carve several small salt dolls of all the things I wish to give up and imagine placing them outside the tent in the rain. As they melt, do I see the imploring look of can't-I-come-back-in-again on the face of Mr. Groton? Nope, and along with the rest, he melts away.

On days like this, I become a turtle and pull in: the top of the wannigan becomes a safe platform to run the stove on, a pot lid under the stove adds insurance against the stove's heat melting the tent's plastic floor. Two cups of water go into the pressure cooker, with a beef or chicken bouillon cube and a cup of short-grain brown rice. When it's done, I pop in the cheese and raisins, give them a stir, and wait for the cheese to melt before declaring dinner ready.

The trick is to have the restraint to let the pressure in the cooker cool down on its own without letting it out sooner. If I don't, the rice tends to be undercooked. It's hard to be patient when you're hungry. I eat with chopsticks out of a wooden bowl. I add lots of Tabasco sauce. This summer, desserts are a problem. I goofed on my chocolate. I thought I'd bought nine one-pound bars of Baker's semisweet chocolate. Not until the first week did I discover that I had bought nine pounds of Baker's *un*sweetened chocolate. I donated it to the bears. Most nights, like tonight, I settle on tea for dessert.

AUGUST 2

Overnight, the storm vanishes. As dramatically dark, brooding, and wet as it had been yesterday, this day is clean and bright with a tailwind. The cool air reminds me of October in Maine. My tent and sleeping bag dry under a light-blue sky. Everything sparkles. Each leaf holds one crystal drop, each drop holds one sun. The ruffled surface of the river crinkles gold and blue. The time I lose in my slow start this morning, I will make up this afternoon.

The light's low angle reveals hundreds of spider webs spread across the willow tops. Why doesn't a spider stick to its own web? They never do, not like people.

¤   ¤   ¤

I set out for Hawk Rapids.

For Captain Back, shooting these rapids proved to be one of the most dramatic events of his trip.

> Early in the morning we pushed into the beginning of the rapids, when the boat was twirled about in whirlpools against the oars; and but for the amazing strength of McKay, who steered, it must inevitably have been crushed against the faces of the protruding rocks. As we entered the defile, the rocks on the right presented a high and perpendicular front, so slaty and regular that it needed no force of imagination to suppose them severed at one great blow from the opposite range; which, craggy, broken, and overhanging, towered in stratified and many-colored masses far above the chafing torrent. There was a deep settled gloom in the abyss— the effect of which was heightened by the hollow roar of the rapid, still in deep shade, and by the screaming of three large hawks, which, frightened from their aerie, were hovering high above the middle of the pass, and gazing fixedly upon the first intruders on their solitude; so that I felt relieved as it were from a load when we once more burst forth into the bright sunshine of day.

Entering Hawk Rapids, the river sweeps down in a sharp right turn. The water accelerates through the middle of the curve. The standing waves and the crush of white water are too powerful for *Loon* to attempt. The cumbersome size of Back's boat forced him to run them. From the hill on the right bank, I chart a route close to shore. I go down to walk its length. I have no McKay to save me. I can only dance my water-spider dance close to shore. There are a few crucial dips and turns. Nothing dangerous. What is dangerous lies a few feet farther from shore: standing waves. They have a deceiving power capable of easing me into them. I wouldn't even sense the danger until *Loon* was on their back and the forward force of the current took charge. Then I'd be in trouble. *Loon* would plow through the curling white top of each successive wave, taking in water until she swung broadside and swamped. I hate thinking about the consequences of poor judgment, but there it is. I walk my route to a small falls. There I'll get out and reconnoiter again.

As I paddle down, I stay in a thin lane to get by the standing waves on my left. Halfway through the rapid at the small falls, to lighten *Loon* I portage the heavier pack a hundred yards ahead. Then I shoot the falls. What I don't see is a rock that wallops *Loon* as we pass through the frothy water. I cringe. I enter the canyon riding the rapid's runoff between the highest rock cliffs I've seen, each side the mirror of the other.

Instead of Back's hawks, two peregrine falcons screech out of their aerie to hover over my descent, feathery dark crosses against the light-blue sky. They scream their high-pitched screams above the rapids' thundering roar. As they escort me out of the rocky defile, the sound rebounds from the high rock walls. I pull over on the left in a small cove below the canyon. Here the river opens out. I climb the canyon wall to look back. The opposite side is lighted up in afternoon light; the red rock, the streaks and clumps of darker rock, are mixed with gray swirls. The peregrines built their nest on a ledge where the sunlight helps heat their eggs and baby-sits the chicks while the parents hunt.

The current running through the canyon is powerful, full of snakelike curves and spins, twists and whirlpools, water reacting to the hidden forces under the surface. I see fish, big ones in that powerful boil of water—they would have to be big fish to live in that current.

I choose a protected hollow, a short walk over grass and sand to the water. As I fill my two pots, I see two insects, not half an inch long,, copulating on my sneaker. They face away from each other and their thoraxes are joined in conjugal bliss: not Shakespeare's beast with two backs, but a mythical-looking creature with one dark body, two heads, twelve legs, and eight gossamer wings. They disagree about the direction of their future happiness. One pulls them across the sneaker's toe, then the other pulls them back. Have I provided the honeymoon bed for future generations of this delicate-looking mayfly? No, they go airborne, flying out over the water still joined. No earthbound orgasm for them.

Compared to yesterday, I spend a quiet evening in preparation for crossing the big lakes, Pelly, and Upper and Lower Garry. I clean some clothes and repack, then rejoin the *Hunchback*, as Quasimodo rescues Esmeralda. If only she would see the love in his heart and not his ugly face.

Several friends gave me envelopes to open along the way. I set the camera up to film my reading of the one from Jim Merrill. The cliff face opposite still glows red, buttered in the evening's late sunlight. The water sparkles. I turn the camera on, walk back to sit down, open and read the poet's letter:

> "Unbeached Canoe"
> *Emptied this evening*
> *of the stuff of survival*
> *for whom do you dance?*

I can think of nothing to say. I look at *Loon*. I can't get his question out of my mind. I let my eyes drift over the water. They begin to dance with the bugs among the last shimmers of the sun's white-gold flecks.

The next morning I get out my maps for a look ahead. More sand, lots more sand, as I paddle toward Pelly Lake. If I don't get a headwind, I should make good time. The day extends the promise of good weather, but I don't trust it. Turning my back to Hawk Rapids, its peregrines, its rumble, I dig my paddle in and pry off the gunwale to move *Loon* into the current where she drifts into the sweeping left turn that carries us out of the canyon's sight.

D
is for dapper, which
is what Mr. Back was.
He wore a Top hat and
a swallowtail coat
all through the Tundra
My hat's off to him. He
did an amazing journey
in 1834. I'm just a
tourist compared to
him. Like to have seen
him in his hat.
viii. iii. 87

D viii. iii.

D *is for Dapper.*

That's what George Back was. He wore a swallowtail coat and a top hat in the tundra.

Sand makes it hard to find the main channel, but enough water flows over the sand bars to float *Loon*. Many terns are fishing this breadth of river: at the apex of their flight they become a flutter of stark white. During the long afternoon, clouds march over the western horizon and pass by me, their shadows silently flowing over the rough landscape. As if it might storm, the sky becomes dark. The terns become candles. The next three rapids are tough. The middle one has a long drop curving right under a high clay bank. Forced away from the inside curve, I plow through three standing waves. If *Loon* didn't have the spray skirt on, she would have swamped. I am proud of her and Denny.

I know a man, much like Denny, who loves a swamp. Both

he and the swamp live in Massachusetts, not far from Walden
Pond. The swamp is bordered by human activity: a railroad,
roads, and a housing development. Every time a certain lady in
the development sees my friend stop his car and unload his canoe,
she calls to him, "If you find anything interesting in there, let me
know. I'd like to see it." It's become a joke between them because
he never tells her what he sees and she never goes into the swamp
to look on her own. Because Thoreau never lived there, the swamp
remains undisturbed by the thousands who go to Walden seeking
a taste of the Thoreauvian spirit. It's just a swamp, nondescript
in every way, until you step into it.

In winter, snowmobiles pass over its frozen surface. Boys
come out on the ice to push over the dead trees. The bird-quarried
and drilled trees left standing resemble unworldly flutes stuck in
the water. The trees on the outside of this dead forest protect
those in the middle. They cut down wind. They muffle road and
house noises, which is important to the herons who nest there.
Owls build their nests there too. The number of dead trees is
dwindling. As long as human traffic remains minimal, the swamp
will survive, as will animal life and vegetation. Often, watching
a heron feed, poised, on one leg, I think how like this bird my
mind is. I dream and ponder, poised, ready to sneak up on a
thought, then quick, the thought arrives, and my mind, like the
heron's neck, cocks back. Strike. The heron wades farther into
the swamp looking for another minnow thought.

I pass the afternoon in relaxed paddling. I practice sitting
straight. I give up after a while and settle back into a more
comfortable position, my mind a sparrow hopping from one thing
to the next, until I notice the two rings I wear. The one on my
left middle finger is a simple silver band I made when I was
nineteen.

The other ring reminds me of geese. It's an aluminum goose
band that fits the last finger on my right hand. In 1970 six of us
arrived at the end of a canoe trip in Eastmain, Quebec. In the

small settlement lived two hundred Cree Indians, a Hudson Bay Post manager, his wife, and three Catholic nuns of the only order that appeals to me: St. Francis of Assisi. We visited the nuns for endless cups of tea and conversation. After two months in the bush, we were eager to talk. They were equally starved to hear news from somewhere else. They lived in the village not to convert, but to help. When I went to say good-bye, Sister Carmine fished in her sewing basket and gave me the goose band. I wear it to remind me of Sister Carmine, St. Francis, and, above either of them, the geese, "God's best dreamers, coming to earth only to rest," as Ezra Pound said.

I paddle around a point ready to quit for the day. In the small scoop of a bay is a loon thrashing its head back and forth trying to swallow the tail end of a large, uncooperative trout. The loon trombones its neck, then swishes it side to side. It lays its head and neck as far back, then as far forward, as possible. Nothing works; the tail of the fish hangs out of its mouth. The loon's absorption in its problem allows me to coast near. As a last resort, the loon dives. Surfacing, the fish is swallowed. More neck tromboning and a hearty yodel show the loon is pleased. Seeing me, the loon harrumphs and gallops across the water's surface, wings flapping, each ungainly step a great splash and water ring, until it is finally airborne. It circles me and flies upriver croaking like a frog.

Perhaps out of deference for its age, Roger Tory Peterson honors the loon with the first page in his bird guide. The oldest known bird, it comes in four variations: the black-and-white common loon, the smaller Arctic loon, the yellow-billed loon, and the colorful red-throated loon.

Instead of camping, I continue. All afternoon my body works. I pick a point, blue in the distance, to paddle toward. If I don't think I'll get caught in wind before I can reach the other shore, I paddle across the mouth of deep bays instead of hugging their shore. It's an endless number of strokes over calm water.

Haven't I seen that rock before? This length of beach? I get out to stretch, the joints of my knees aching. I brew a cup of coffee in the canoe. I stop in the evening, estimating I've paddled fifteen miles. I'm approaching Pelly Lake. Maybe in the next day or two I'll be there.

Pitching the tent, I smell an odd aroma. The few smells in the tundra stay close to the ground. This one doesn't. It clashes. By following it in the light wind to the top of the ridge, I locate the source. Among the gray boulders lies a dead caribou. Its stomach is swollen. The hair is peeling away from the skin in large furry patches. The exposed skin has dried to a dark, leathery brown. I can't see any wound. The head rests on a rock, as if in dying it chose to put it there. No large animal has touched it, but flies cover the body, especially the head, buzzing and landing, walking, tasting; like hundreds of tiny black periods, they mark the death of the caribou and the birth of new generations of flies. The lips are drawn back in a frozen grimace, exposing teeth and red gums. The gums have been worked over by the flies, and glisten from open sores. Like the small sparrow I found at Beechey Lake, nothing is missing but the eye. Eyelashes hang over the vacant socket, as if expecting the eye to reappear, the head to rise, and the legs to bend, lifting the caribou up so it can shake off this bad dream and amble away.

What is it like to die? Do you know it's happening? Do you know an hour before? Not at all? Is my father dead? Will I see him again? The day I left, I kidded with him about an ancient Egyptian belief that says when a man dies his soul is weighed in a scale opposite a feather; if the soul weighs more than the feather, he won't get to the next world. I said he'd better go on a diet or he wouldn't get to heaven. He shot right back, "I don't want to die-yet," running the last two words together. What an odd good-bye: wishing each other luck, not knowing if we'd survive the summer.

I stand up and shake. I go walking to collect alder sticks for a fire. I like a fire at night, even if it's not dark out. The best twigs are old ones lying on the ground. Dead ones attached to the alder bush are hard to break off, but both kinds light quickly and burn hot. The weathered wood has a creamy texture smooth to the touch and a blue-gray, white color. I hold up the bottom edge of my anorak to collect twigs. I find an abandoned bird nest for kindling. I curl myself around the small fire feeding it, breathing its scent, watching each stick turn into a red eye of coal. When a man dies his soul is weighed in a scale opposite a feather. I poke the fire and in the ashes watch coals jump alive. For one brief moment, they glow red before dimming. One brief moment: that's all we get.

I start late the next day and continue paddling into the evening. I want to take advantage of this string of good weather while it lasts. If there's a storm later on, I could be held up crossing the big lakes. I find crossing large bodies of open water nerve-wracking.

As I finish dinner in *Loon*, a light meal of leftover rice and bannock, the sun does a split on the high pile of cumulus clouds in the southeast, turning their full white heads even whiter and their lower halves a dusty purple and alizarin crimson. They are two separate sunsets, created in a fluke of low-angle sun. I remember my night-paddles earlier in the summer. Each night gets a little darker now. Around the middle of August darkness will return. I hold my breath. An occasional birdcall anchors the silence, focuses my attention. The call leaves a deeper silence behind. I am alone. A small Lapland longspur flies across the river thirty yards ahead, a black speck, its flight path climbing up the air, coasting down, climbing up, coasting down. The river runs silent between two black shores, a liquid mirror reflecting essences. There is no image of *Loon*, only twin ribbons of water trailing off either side of the bow. The fading circles of my paddle strokes are darkest where the small central whirlpool spins. The clouds are a diffuse glow of upside-down cumulus. Passing feathers and bugs are black dust on the river surface. A duck flying up-river is a dark shadow.

Slowly, like a new taste, the river reveals itself. Am I not living all my own cool opposites? Am I not stitching myself into this night with each needle-like paddle stroke?

The night circles itself. I don't know if I'm waking up or going to sleep. I try to notice the river change color, but miss it. The water turns black, a tarnished silver mirror. Soon the sun, with rays of pale-orange sherbet, tosses back the indefiniteness of the last few hours. I camp, and try to sleep before the sun's heat on the tent forces me awake.

Pelly Lake can't be far ahead. When I get up, I take a walk inland away from where I've camped to see if I can establish my position. I amble for several miles, as much for the sheer pleasure of walking as to find out where I am. I see hills off to the east, running in a northerly direction. The river opens up to the north-east and turns to the right. I think I see the open water of Pelly Lake, named by Back after Sir Henry Pelly, one of the first governors of the Hudson's Bay Company and a patron of Back's expedition.

As I turn to leave the ridge, I see the oval shape at my feet, half buried in the pebbles and hard clay. I pick up the scraper, a beautiful, ancient tool. It's about four inches long. The exposed side is covered with spots of lichen. I dream of finding things like this. Holding it, I try to imagine the first hands that held it, that decided this dusty red stone would do. I think of the hands that held the larger piece of stone this smaller oval was flaked out of. I imagine the woman's hands that used it to soften skins. Was this a valued scraper? Was it discarded, or dropped on a march? Is this the tip of a midden belonging to one family, or ten? Ovals and circles, Inuit life revolved around those forms: the kayak, a pinched oval; tents, caches, soapstone lamps, igloos, seasons, sun, moon, circles of myth, cycles of life. Progress isn't everybody's idea of a good time.

If you live circles instead of lines, you live for repetition, not for novelty and newness. I sit, my legs straight in front of me, and use the scraper to push sand. I run its edge along the palm of my left hand. I regard it carefully. I feel the concentration of the tundra's spirit in it. I think about the drawers and drawers of scrapers at the Smithsonian Institution in Washington, D. C. — locked up in the dark, occasionally studied, but because of their sheer numbers never individually cherished. I could report my find to them or the Yellowknife Museum. They would add it to the long list of locations they will get to someday, or I could take it in and save them the expense of flying to what may not be a major site.

Or I could take the scraper home with me where it would be lovingly cared for.

I place the scraper by my right thigh. I stand up and dust off my pants and walk away. I will never forget the electric feeling of finding the scraper, holding it, and the pleasure I've had dreaming about the person who shaped it and the one who used it. I leave it on the land, in an oval of time, a concentration of spirit— as a center of all that moves and all that is still.

I enter Pelly Lake in the afternoon. The river current and wind run at loggerheads and kick up whitecaps. I keep *Loon*'s bow slightly off the wind at an angle to the waves. Individually each wave is no threat, but it's the doubles and triplets that worry me. I ride *Loon* like a seesaw, leaning back to keep the bow from burying itself in oncoming waves, then rocking forward to paddle.

When I stop there seems to be no place to camp except behind a wall of boulders pushed up by the ice. I find a place for the tent on a rocky, hard-packed clay pan, behind which stretches a plain of knotty women's heads and water. For the moment, the wind is on the other side of the rock wall, whistling through the cracks.

Carrying *Loon* up from the river, to get her on grass for the night, my right foot hits a stone and I fall on her. She lands on a sharp rock followed by my full weight. I put a three-inch tear in her side where the white of the topside meets the black, her most vulnerable spot. I think of all the rapids we've shot, the rocks we hit and missed, and on land I punch a hole in her. I'll be here until I fix it.

Working with resins terrifies me. My brother and Denny have warned me about their toxicity. They've turned me into a chicken. Fortunately, Denny has given me a "cold-cure" type of resin that sets up in any weather, any temperature, even underwater, but I can't do anything until tomorrow.

Outside the tent, clouds rush by. The weather turns grisly and cold. When this storm breaks, it is going to be a doozy. The clouds are as dark and thick as the flying monkeys that chase Dorothy and her friends in *The Wizard of Oz*. After dinner, the storm opens up with blasts of wind and crashes of thunder and rain. I drift to sleep imagining my tent is a small egg in a nest of thunderstorms.

Sometime in the night I wake up. I feel the drizzle falling over miles of tundra. A wolf howls. There is no answering call. Low and high notes, long drawn out notes, bore into me, tangling me up in peculiar feelings. I doubt the wolf would come near my tent, but the tent wall is paper thin. I think about how immense and utterly indifferent this land and the wolf are to us, how afraid we are of wide-open space. The wolf is an emissary to us from the land and more like us than we allow. She may not look like us, but in our deepest rhythms, our deepest organs, our red blood, we are identical. I listen to her howling. The land reverberates. The howls reverberate in me, lifting my senses out of the tent to spread over the tundra along with the night, and the drizzle.

¤ ¤ ¤

The next morning the wind has died. It is still gray and drizzling. In between cups of tea I fix the tear in *Loon*. The resin hardened even in this weather. As penance for my clumsiness, I set out in the rain and paddle along the north shore of Pelly Lake in and out of small, pancake islands barely visible above the water. As I come to an esker posing as an island, a caribou with a large rack of antlers appears on the ridgeline. It trots down toward shore. When it sees me, it snorts and clatters among the rocks along the beach waving its head as if agreeing with something. It disappears around a corner.

Reaching the same corner, I see exposed water ahead. The wind is returning. I set out anyway, to get at least to the first big bay I'll have to cross. But when the breeze becomes a headwind, I decide to spend the afternoon doing something other than paddling. I tuck into a cove and discover I am not its first visitor.

Over the last weeks, I've seen several old campsites: a ring of rocks for a fire, the odd bit of paper or tape, some small relic indicating modern travelers, but nothing more. Most people respect the land enough to clean up after themselves. What I find here is a travesty: a full-blown monument complete with bronze plaque. Climbing up from the small crescent beach to the goose grass, I see the name of the expedition and the year of its triumph emblazoned on the ground. Stones from the size of grapefruits to small watermelons spell out each four-foot-long letter:

PELLY LAKE EXPEDITION
1979

They would have saved themselves work if they'd said "trip" instead of "expedition." The intervening eight years have done nothing to dim the message. I walk up a nearby knoll to a cairn. Screwed into the face of a large elevated piece of pink granite is a bronze plaque:

SIR JOHN HENRY PELLY, BARONET
MARCH 31, 1777–AUGUST 13, 1852

To recognise an historical contribution
to developing Canada
in his role as Governor,
Hudson's Bay Company,
1822–1852

ERECTED AUGUST 13, 1977
BY THE PELLY LAKE
CANOE EXPEDITION:

DAVID F. PELLY   BRIAN PELLY
THOMAS A. MAWHINNEY   PETER W. DION

A genealogical canoe trip to commemorate Henry Pelly. The lake already bears the Pelly name. Everyone who cares about the history of the north is familiar with Henry Pelly, the Hudson's Bay Company, and their northern legacy. Many monuments have been erected in the North, but they commemorate something unique, remarkable, heroic, or tragic. They commemorate consequence. This is just plain ego.

Walking back to *Loon* I notice what a pretty cove she's in. She sits on a thin smile of sand, the curve of the crescent moon. The lake's far shore is a barely visible line of gray and dark blue, interrupted by a swath of flesh color, the exposed face of an esker. I pull out my pack and set up my tent. As long as the weather continues windy, I'm stuck here. No bugs are out in this weather. With the tent door facing away from the wind, I don't need the mosquito netting zipped up. I bake banana bread in the pressure cooker, one of two premixed packages I brought. I brew a cup of coffee to drink with it. The flamingo, stuck in the ground ten feet away, bobs and twists on its one metal leg. Over the summer it's brought me pleasure. It's companionable. A ground squirrel appears, first sniffing the flamingo's tail, then approaching the tent. The closer it comes, the quieter I am. It runs off, then returns, a little closer each time. I load the camera. Soon I'm filming the squirrel eating out of my hand. I like to think this is the first step toward my being a modern St. Francis, but it's more likely proof that a ground squirrel's stomach can overcome its fears.

Restless, I take a walk toward a frown of hill behind my camp. The loose rock is dark, almost black in this dampness. Streaked with iron red, it slips easily under foot. I turn downhill to a pond where three Arctic loons are holding court. The wind doesn't bother them. If they're not bobbing on the waves, they're hidden in the troughs. They yap loudly as they dive underwater. One runs across the water, wings out as though flashing the other two.

The loons crisscross the surface of the small pond, exercising their voices with a variety of calls, yodels, tremolos, and cries, ranging from the almost human to the truly eerie. Because the loon's multiple voices implied that a number of spirits lived in it, the Inuit regarded the loon as a powerful bird. In certain communities a shaman donned a hat, coat, and vest made of loon feathers to invoke the bird as his spirit guide during his travels to other worlds.

As the front passes, the wind shifts to a tailwind. Early the next morning, I leave this cove and its monument. In this uncorrupted wilderness, one of the last in North America, the cove is a natural shape in a litany of tundra phenomena. As innocently, as reverently as the monument may have been erected, it marks the intrusive spirit of human beings.*

I pass more pancake islands, the nesting ground for snow geese and the feeding ground for gulls. Crossing the mouth of the first big bay, I paddle by three tiny islands, mere piles of rock in the water. The bays of Pelly Lake reach inland fifteen to twenty miles from the lake's main body. The distant views are alluring, lots of sand and low hills. Anyone loving roundness and smooth lines that flirt with the sky and end in suggestions of hidden gullies would feel drawn to these bays. After the next bay I'll enter Garry Lake, where I want to stop at an old island mission site.

The Pelly and Garry lakes were once home to many Inuit families. Because of its remoteness, no trader bothered to venture here. The same was true of missionaries. Until Father Joseph Buliard chose this area for his mission in 1949, no one had been here to Christianize these families. It was too difficult to reach.

On my map, I've gotten as far as the letter *E* of "Lake" in the words "Pelly Lake." It shows a land bridge connecting the mainland to an offshore island. Normally I would paddle around the island's outside edge, then back to shore. With this wind behind me, I try something different. Portaging over the thin strip of land would save paddling into a crosswind. I paddle into the horseshoe bay and am soon out of any wind. The sun feels good on my back. The height of the land bridge prevents me from seeing if the plan will work until I climb the bank. The top is as flat and as straight as a railroad bed. The other side drops off. I'll have little trouble going downhill with *Loon*. It's 150 yards. I carry everything over. As I load *Loon* with my gear, I see the getaway is tougher than it looked, shallow and full of rocks. Hi, ho, *Loon!* I get my feet wet, but soon we are zinging parallel to the main shore. What look like canoer cairns turn out to be the real thing: by coming this way, I've stumbled on a group of half

---

*In 1990 I was told the monument no longer exists.

a dozen *inukshuks*. Climbing on the rock to visit them I find three meat caches, piles of stone where caribou were buried for protection from scavengers. Looking into one, I see the bones. The thick covering of lichen on all parts of the *inukshuks* indicates their age. Nothing grows quickly in the lichen world. None of these totems stand taller than my thigh, yet, especially from the water, they are magnetic. Maybe they were navigation aides. Maybe fish were dried on lines hung between them. Maybe they were used as hunting blinds. Maybe there was a deeper meaning.

Although no Inuit live on the land today, they inhabited this immense slice of tundra for at least five thousand years. Their fully rounded civilization, older than mine, surviving in this inhospitable terrain, left no physical mark taller than these stones. They viewed the land as a community. They were one piece of it. For thousands of years its mysteries and the returning cycle of seasons remained the inheritance of each generation. Until we arrived it was the only life the people knew. Circles and ovals. My culture sees the land as commodity. The history of my culture is a straight line called progress. We depend on industry to supply our needs but have forgotten what industry depends on. The older culture has been overtaken, but ours has yet to prove its superiority.

Between the time George Back first encountered the Inuit and the 1950s when the last families were moved off the land by government order—roughly 120 years—a whole culture, loving, warring, starving, yet surviving, was ruined.

Minik was an eight-year-old Greenland Eskimo when the polar explorer Robert Peary brought him, his father Qisuk, and four other Eskimos to New York. The year was 1897, three years before Peary's first attempt to reach the North Pole. Along with barrels of bones and ancient artifacts taken from Greenland, Peary proudly handed the six Eskimos to the American Museum of Natural History in New York. When things soured in the press, Peary stated that the Eskimos had asked to come, although that was not what he said originally. These Eskimos were in New York to further Peary's reputation and as specimens for the museum.

Within nine months, four of the Eskimos died of pneumonia and Minik's father lay close to death. Members of the museum staff, under the direction of Franz Boas, coolly studied Qisuk's last weeks with his son. When Qisuk died, the museum director, Walter Jessup, appointed the groundskeeper Minik's guardian. Robert Peary had washed his hands of the whole affair, refusing to speak to Minik, or to provide compensation to the families of the dead men. The museum held a funeral on its grounds for Minik's benefit to show him that his father received a proper Christian burial, but to the boy this was only another new and baffling ceremony. As the coffin was lowered into the ground, the assembled museum staff gave their blessings to the deceased.

Years passed. Minik remained in New York. As the ward of the groundskeeper, he had the run of the museum. He was fifteen when he found the glass case in the museum's basement with a skeleton hanging in it. The label on the case read "The Skeleton of Qisik, a Polar Eskimo."*

As I paddle away from the evocative stones, I pass the mouth of the east bay before the narrows dividing Pelly Lake from Garry Lake. At the narrows, the lake splits around an island, briefly becoming a river again as the higher lake drains into the lower, larger Garry Lake. I choose to run the island's left side. The river tilts away from the island toward a point near the shore. Entering the short rapid, the water, drawn taut, develops folds like a poorly tucked sheet. I drift into it, *Loon* slides easily over the creases. I dart left, then paddle right and I'm through. I camp at the base of the rapid.

*For a detailed account of this story, see: Ken Harper, *Give Me My Father's Body: The Life of Minik, the New York Eskimo* (Frobisher Bay: Blacklead Books, 1986).

Where there's a rapid, there are fish. I set up my fly rod and, within several casts, catch two trout. Instead of frying them, I boil the fish to save what little oil I have left.

After dinner I work on the Tundrabet, and later I finish *The Hunchback of Notre Dame*. The thought that Quasimodo would go to the crypt for criminals to die beside the already hanged Esmeralda, their skeletons forever united, haunts me.

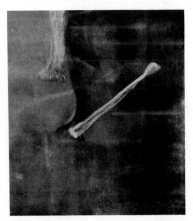

E *is for eating.*

That's what everybody up here is doing to one another. Bones all over the place. I saw where a wolf had wedged the leg bone of a caribou between two rocks. That's how he broke it open to get at the marrow.

Awakened by a salvo of geese-calling, I get an early start toward Garry Lake. Louder than the rapid, they fire away, one pure complaint after another, unmusical and unpleasing. Aldo Leopold may have listened breathlessly to "goose music" as they flew over his head in Wisconsin announcing spring, but this morning's group has fallen drastically out of tune or I'm grumpy.

There is a headwind. The sky is gray. If the weather gets worse, I won't make it to Father Buliard's mission house today.

Throughout the summer I have observed different busy workers, but the busiest is the bumblebee. While there's light, they work, and for more than a month it's been light all the time. From the tent I hear them *zing* by, a big heavy sound. This afternoon one comes alongside *Loon*. The gray weather and strong headwind might have hidden it, but as I lean forward over my stroke, one appears in front of my nose. It moves over to the lane next to mine. No bumblebee in its right mind would go to work into a strong headwind. This bee must be headed home. It's as large as my thumbnail, its pollen buckets like tiny taillights. We work hard to maintain momentum. The small black shape pushes forward, slowly at first, then faster. I strain to keep it in sight, marveling at the large bee body under a swirling congregation of gray clouds, flying over dark waves and against a thin black horizon, drawn forward by the magnetic power of home. I'm alone, but not unaccompanied. An hour longer and cracks appear in the clouds creating irregular patterns of blue sky. Over another hour, the blue sky disperses the gray clouds.

I leave the river narrows and enter Garry Lake with a stiff breeze behind me. Traveling with the following waves seems easier than paddling into them, but turns out to be just as trying. Over my shoulder, I constantly check the angle of the stern in relation to the next wave. To watch the waves behind me and steer *Loon* at the same time is disconcerting. I see the island, a high esker headland, but to reach the cabin I'll have to travel the island's long west side. Not until I angle around a rock point can I relax. From the island's uniform and undulating surfaces, and numerous patches of exposed, flesh-colored sand, I see the green covering as a grass sheet with tears in it revealing a sand body underneath. In front of me is a crescent beach, the longest and most handsome I've seen.

From the beach the land rises, and Father Buliard's cabin sits in a fold a hundred yards up, and an equal number back, from shore. Seeing four walls and a roof, a human habitation—not a den, a hole in the earth, or a nest—is a shock. After beaching *Loon* I walk up. Considering the small cabin hasn't been lovingly lived in since 1956, it looks in good shape. Bernie took a slide in 1976 showing a cross on top of the cabin; a stovepipe sits there now. Like a wary animal, I circle the cabin before entering it. Several different people, at various times, have used it as a base for fishing and trapping: rubber gloves, used cans of motor oil, snowmobile parts, rusty traps, spools of nylon fishing line, nets, and a ripped drysuit lie discarded on the ground, or are visible through the windows on the cabin floor. Turning the corner to the back of the cabin, I see a sparrow struggling in the dust. It stops to gather itself, but even in this brief moment, I see its strength failing. It is caught in the mesh of a clear monofilament fishnet. Thrown out as garbage, partially buried over time, the discarded net could still catch. The bird did not perceive its threat, and while pecking for food in the dirt it got snared. It's difficult for me to assure the poor thing of my good intentions. I hold the wings to its body with my left hand while the jackknife in my right cuts at the plastic manacles. The sparrow's body trembles. Finally it's free. As it flies off, the rapid drumming whir of its wings is all the thanks I get.

I didn't think I would, but I decide to stay. The weather is good and the view from the front of the cabin breathtaking. If this had been my mission, I would have felt close to God. Facing south, the cabin's three-room length runs east to west. The smaller of the cabin's two main rooms—the middle room, or snow room—is attached to the largest room by a door to the right inside the front door. I enter the main room through the connecting door. The floors of each room are buried in animal droppings, sand and dirt, and human debris. Some of the more recent humans have written dates and names on the walls, others have drawn pictures. The rooms' windows are blown out, shards of broken glass litter the floor and the ground outside. Over time, shelves have been ripped down. At other times people have jerryrigged them back up. Someone nailed a sardine can to a wall as a candle holder. Not much remains as Father Buliard left it.

More fishing net, rubber gloves, traps, fox skeletons, and nylon rope lie tangled in heaps. Several of the priest's special Bibles translated into the Inuit language have been translated again, this time into bedding for mice and reading material for the wind. The rain and snow have thumbed them with wet fingers, swelling the tattered pages to twice their original size. The smallest room at the west end must have been the storeroom. Now it's a wreck. Human scavengers have peeled off its tarpaper to get at the lumber underneath. The remaining shell of a space has become a dump for anything empty, broken, and worn out. Not that everyone puts their junk in the dump—much of it lies in expanding circles around the cabin.

Many of my friends don't want to see cabins, or other people, when they travel, but to me there is something compelling about coming upon a house in an immense wilderness. Maybe it's because I travel alone. Houses want to be lived in, cleaned up, even ratty ones like this. Cleaning up the middle room becomes my late-afternoon task. I find the stub end of a broom in the junk outside, even a rusty old dustpan. My sweeping evokes *chee-chee-cheed* protests from the ground squirrels living under the cabin. One pokes its head up through a hole to scold me in person. The room's three self-standing shelves are covered in rotten linoleum. I rip the linoleum off, ball it up, and heave it out the door. Later I'll deposit it in the side shed along with whatever other large pieces of trash I can pick up.

At an early age, Joseph Buliard felt chosen for the priesthood. He left France to fulfill his calling in the Arctic, eventually settling here on his own among the district's Inuit families.

I've never been in favor of the missionary spirit. It is a bitter fruit that has destroyed many cultures.

I grew up with missionaries, though not Catholic ones. Down the hill from our house, my parents fixed up an old barn, converting the hayloft into an apartment that they rented to young couples attending Gordon College Seminary. In exchange for inexpensive rent, the boarders helped my mother in the house and around the yard. There were many couples over the years. It was here that they began putting into practice what later would pull them to the ends of the earth: my three sisters, my brother, and I were going to be their first converts. Away from their homes in the Midwest for the first time, they found themselves living in Unknown Country (Manchester-by-the-Sea), surrounded by Thick Forest (a few well-spaced white pines and hemlocks), due to the goodwill of the Local Headman and his Woman (my father and mother).

Ah, Mrs. Harmony said to herself, there's one now, pushing his bike up the hill. "Hello, there. Don't they call you Robby?" she says. In a year, she will be somewhere else saying, "Aren't you the one they call Abujonju?"

"Yes,' I answer.

"Would you like a chocolate chip cookie? I just finished baking some," she says.

"Sure." I lean my bike on the railing and run right up.

"How about some milk to go with them?" coaxes Mrs. Harmony. She's never done this before.

"Yes, please."

"How old are you, Robby?"

"Nine."

"Have you ever heard of God?" she asks.

"Yeah, sure. That's what my dad calls the man over on Eagle Head who has lots of money and a big house. May I have another cookie?"

"Certainly. No, I mean God, who made heaven and hell."

"Oh," I say, munching the cookie around the chocolate chips first, saving the chips for last. "Not really."

"The way to him is through Jesus Christ. The same way," Mrs. Harmony says with a rush of inspiration, "the cookie gets to your mouth. Have another." As I bring the cookie to my mouth, she interrupts. "See, your hand brings the cookie to you, the same way Jesus Christ, and belief in him, can bring you to God."

"What if I don't want to believe?"

"But you should."

"Why?"

"It will make you feel good."

"Oh, but Mrs. Bender said it was Jesus Christ that should be in my stomach, along with the cookies and milk. Not God."

"Who's Mrs. Bender?" asks Mrs. Harmony, slightly taken aback.

"She's the lady who lived here before you. She'd talk to my brother and me the way you are now. Once she made brownies for my sisters. We never understood why she couldn't enjoy her food without talking about God. May I have one more before I go? They're awfully good."

"Sure," says Mrs. Harmony.

"Thanks a lot. It's nice to meet you. If you ever want to talk to God, maybe I can get my dad to drive us over to Eagle Head."

The men were different. They carried pictures, either black and white or colored ones, of a very unhappy looking man in a robe with thorns on his head. Or diagrams. I liked the diagrams because they looked like improbable geometry.

Enlisted by the Head Woman, I'd be helping mow the lawn, or splitting wood, or raking leaves with the barn's current male occupant. Before long the young missionary would find an excuse to start a conversation. We'd be chatting about leaves, or the weather, until inevitably the subject of God came up. As I got older, instead of saying, "I don't know," I'd say, "I don't believe." Often I would just go back to work. My family had their own belief and liked to let other people have theirs.

This was the first and only mission built in the remote Garry Lake district. Before Father Buliard arrived, the Inuit families here had to travel long distances if they were interested in hearing about a different form of belief from the one they practiced. More likely, if they made the arduous trip, they were interested in the white man's tools, line, fishhooks, guns, and bullets. When Father Buliard arrived, they could easily get the goods they wanted, plus a new belief. Perhaps they found they could get the one more easily when they had the other.

In 1955 after a year went by with no word from Buliard, a plane was sent from Baker Lake to pick him up. The photographer, Richard Harrington, was in Baker Lake when the plane returned. He told me Father Buliard wasn't making much sense— "Too much time on his own"—but Buliard soon recovered and returned to his mission. After that no one on the outside saw him again. Some believe he fell through the ice while checking his nets. Others believe he was murdered by three disgruntled Inuit who either did not appreciate his breaking up their traditional way of life, or for some more immediate, practical reason. The three men suspected of the murder died of starvation the following year. For the Inuit to have murdered him sounds out of character, unless it was a particularly grievous thing Father Buliard did to provoke them. Another story is that a group of Norwegian canoeists found the remains of a skeleton around an old sled on one of the islands in Garry Lake before they knew the Father Buliard story. When they heard it they returned, but could never find the island again.

By suppertime, to save putting the tent up, I move into the cabin's middle room. I even air out an old mattress. I fix up a broken chair and nail a board under the room's one window for a thin table. What fun to be in a house with a table and chair! Not an arm's length behind the table is my "kitchen," the highest of three standing shelves. In this shelf I notice a rectangle of white cotton fabric that I suppose Father Buliard used as a hot plate. I don't give it another thought, and cook my rice.

The next day is nicer, but there's still a strong wind. Too bad, because I want to cross these lakes soon. Paddling long distances on open water is one of the worst aspects of the trip, especially alone. As I brew a cup of tea in the afternoon, my eye lights on that piece of white fabric. What is it? I take out my jackknife. Gently I pry out a small bundle. Tiny stitches run along three sides of the bag. Judging from the nail heads in the shelf, and the rotten linoleum I ripped off, this is old, probably from Father Buliard's time. I couldn't have found something of his, could I? In the thirty years since his disappearance, surely all the people passing through here have taken everything of value. In an Arctic cabin it's hard to hide anything, let alone for that long. Why would Father Buliard want to hide anything?

One side of the package is smooth, the other has indentations. Something the size of a quarter floats loose in the bag. Instead of cutting the stitching, I slit the bag down the middle. As I lift out the contents, I see a marble slab cracked in two. After fitting the halves together, I sit transfixed looking at five small Roman crosses cut in the light-gray and cream-colored marble. A shallow hole is carved slightly above the lower two crosses, and in it sits a miniature bundle expertly tied up in red thread. A wafer-thin piece of marble the size of a quarter fits over this hole. A secret, inside another secret, sewn up in a bag, flipped over and hidden in a shelf. Is there a note, an explanation inside? I carefully cut the thread. Inside the thread is a piece of cotton. Inside the cotton is a sliver of bone, an explanation of sorts.

I go for a long walk over the island. The sun is setting, the wind dying. I come to a stop at a boulder on the island's west edge. I watch a gull change from white to black as it flies in the face of the orange sun. His secret. Wasn't it the focal point of his life? The gull shoots out from in front of the sun, turning back to white, and scuds off on the wind. I should put it all back, but I can't replace the linoleum. Like the scraper, wherever the marble slab goes, it falls out of context. All I can decide is that something is being asked of the small slab, and of me. But what?

In bed, the choices boil around in my head. The wind circles the cabin like a conscience. It rattles little pieces of paper and small metal things in the room next door as if it searches for something. I think of Rasmussen's recorded myth about the *inua* of a dead person flying to the moon. How when you can't see her, the moon is down on earth redistributing *inua* into other forms, even into other human forms.

In the morning I know what to do. I take the small marble slab outside. I hide the slab in a place that should please him. Now this half of himself is with him in the land. Anywhere is the center of the earth, equally visible to the moon and the sun.

I think of another tundra native, Salatha, and his talk with a priest about heaven:

> "Tell me, Father," Salatha asked, "what is the white man's Heaven?"
>
> "It is the most beautiful place in the world," the priest replied.
>
> Then Salatha said:
>
> "Tell me, Father, is it like the land of the little sticks when the ice has left the lake? Are the great musk-oxen there? Are the hills covered with flowers? There, will I see the caribou everywhere I look? Are the lakes blue with the sky of summer? Is every net full of great, fat whitefish? Is there room for me in this land, like our land, the Barrens? Can I camp anywhere and not find that someone else has camped? Can I feel the wind and be like the wind? Father, if your Heaven is not like all these, leave me alone in my land, the land of little sticks."

The next morning is quiet with no wind. Gray clouds dispense a thin white light. Occasionally stronger bands of light stream down to skip and glint on the water like coins. An owl glides over the point I will paddle toward. Noiselessly it hunts, crisscrossing the edge of the bank leading down to the beach where I stand frozen by *Loon*. The mothlike quality of its wings and its pendulum flight increase the silence. I leave the island, the beach, and Father Buliard's cabin to rejoin the mainland on the north shore. I hug it as I paddle toward my crossing of the largest of the three lakes.

The ratio of water to land is about sixty-forty. On the map the white parts are land. The blue parts, the water—pond, lake, stream, river, or puddle—makes up the majority. The land resembles a piece of paper after a young dog has finished chewing it.

I can choose not to cross the lake and paddle a mile of open water to the south shore. However, I'll have to paddle the circumference of the south shore to the lake's outlet. If a north wind arrives, I'm pinned. Another alternative is to paddle straight across from here to the narrows, a several-hour paddle. Or I can go north and use small bits of shredded island as protected stepping-stones for a quarter of the way across. The far shore is a dark-blue blur rising a thin scratch above the water horizon. There's nothing high enough on the opposite shore to give me a bearing. I try to appraise the weather, but it's not revealing its future intentions. Gray sky. Calm. In the end, my nervousness about missing this calm period, and not wanting to get weatherbound on the south shore, or where I stand, sets *Loon* on a compromise course between paddling straight across and swinging north to pick up the chain of islands. I'll paddle a curve, a slow arc into the lake until the islands line up behind me. Then I'll travel straight on to the entrance of Lower Garry Lake.

I start in the afternoon, after a bowl of tea. There is no point in hurrying, as I'd only wear myself out. I remember that a river flowing into Garry Lake had been named last year after Eric Morse. Until his death, he had been the dean of Canadian wilderness canoeing. Before modern canoeing attracted a wide audience, Morse and his friends traveled Arctic rivers. Starting in the 1940s to retrace old Canadian fur trade routes, Eric (and later his wife, Pamela) continued taking long trips. Canada has named a river for him, although a larger one would have been more fitting.

On our way north in 1976, Bernie and I stopped in Ottawa at the invitation of a friend who put us in touch with Mr. Morse. On hearing we were headed for the Back River, he generously offered to take us to lunch at the Redeau Club. Two other gentlemen joined us: Mr. L. A. C. O. Hunt, a retired Hudson Bay man, and Graham Rolley, an archaeologist. They regaled us with their stories. The club's atmosphere was reserved, but by the time the entrees arrived, the laughter erupting from our table set us apart. Halfway through lunch Mr. Hunt, a stout man with a large twinkle in his eye, let it be known he'd recently flown over Hudson Bay in a cargo carrier. The plane detoured two hundred miles from its course to land. Both Mr. Morse's and Mr. Rolley's ears pricked up. (Mr. Rolley had spent much of his career in Hudson Bay and a small cluster of islands there were named for him.)

"Yes," said Mr. Hunt. "I couldn't come that near your islands without paying them a visit." Mr. Morse looked sideways at his friends, as if he knew what was coming.

"Really?" Mr. Rolley remarked.

"Yes," went on Mr. Hunt. "How could I pass up an opportunity to pee on one?"

Mr. Rolley was first to laugh.

The conversation turned to the best way to cook a char. Having no idea what a char was, Bernie and I had no opinion. There was one advocate for boiling, one for frying, and one who saw benefits to both. None of them was subdued in espousing his preference. When he brought dessert, the waiter quietly pointed out to Mr. Morse that other tables had remarked on our volume. Mr. Morse ignored him, but gracefully changed the subject by encouraging Bernie and me to help ourselves to more hot chocolate sauce for the ice cream.

"You won't have any of that where you're going."

I watch the calm water of the big lake and the activity on it. Insects of one description or another land or launch themselves, or flutter helplessly on the surface of this immense liquid airfield. I come to a black stripe of bugs three inches wide and a hundred yards long, floating in an irregular pattern the way seaweed is left on a beach after high tide. They are small black bugs with gossamer wings folded back along their bodies. Those still alive, not standing on the backs of their dead companions, hold themselves stiff-legged off the water as if they find themselves on a journey they had not asked for. One or two launch straight up, where I lose their delicate form against the gray fabric of the clouds. A large trout, relaxed and enjoying itself, lolls along the edge of the insect stripe, lifting first one side of its head, then the other, to suck them in.

I see moths stuck in the center of expanding circles, broken whirligigs fluttering on the water. More fish rise. Every so often I take half a dozen long, hard strokes, thinking these will get me across faster. Around *Loon* the world seems turned into water, sky, and a thin strip of earth. I try not to think of the water depth, or how inconvenient tipping over would be if the weather changed. In this gray world, the light-blue spray cover is encouraging. The afternoon wears on and the clouds begin trailing soft veils of rain; a few drape down as far as the water's surface. Several at a time pass *Loon* on all sides. They make a hissing sound as the rain touches the lake. I feel like the small, stiff-legged insects: an accidental tourist in a world where nothing is solid. I try not to imagine the mist will turn to heavy rain or that a wind will rise. I try to concentrate on the things in the water around me, the water lines off the bow, the unusual light . . .

I think of my dad. He looked bad after his operation. He lay on his back. His voice was faint. His hand felt weak and light in mine. There was no sheet. He wore his hospital gown, the open-back kind that comes only to the knees. I didn't like standing over him, so I sat on the windowsill. For a minute we looked at each other. He didn't want to talk, so I did. As I spoke, he sat up at the edge of the bed, his feet dangling. In that moment he looked like a child.

I continued to talk. He pushed himself up, wavering onto his feet. My voice trailed off. I asked if I could help, but his left hand waved me away. Weakly he apologized and began to walk toward the bathroom in the corner, stopping often to gather himself. His mussed white hair stuck out at odd angles. He was thin. All I could think of as I watched him was Lear on the heath, his rage spent, his world shrunk so small everything in it was genuine. It took him ten minutes to cross the floor. I remember saying to myself, "If he can do that, what I'm about to do is a piece of cake."

I've lined up the islands behind me. I straighten my course. I should land south of the inlet into Lower Garry Lake. The new shore is visible, but I won't be there for forty more minutes. As if a tailor snipped it from a larger bolt, the gray clouds slip away exposing a clear, cobalt-blue evening. The day's first direct sunlight wakes up the colors along the approaching shoreline: mustard rocks, rose-madder slabs of outcrop, burnt-umber tundra, thalo-green willows, and small corn-yellow patches of sand snap to attention. Nothing indicates where I have landed, but that's okay; I've landed.

Standing on shore, looking back, I stretch, walk around, jump up and down a few times on terra firma. I get out the map and begin checking for landmarks, interpolating my position. I should be a mile, maybe two, south of the outlet leading to the next lake. I'll leisurely paddle the shore until I reach it. I'll know if I've gone too far north if I come to a big island at the end of the mainland. After eating some cheese, I'm off.

The water is calm. The low, raking light is made more dramatic by the edge of departing clouds that cover the sky from the east up to my zenith. I paddle one mile. I paddle two, all the time twisting the map around and inspecting the shoreline to find a fit. My confidence begins to rub thin; I don't like to think about what's underneath. Perhaps I did land north of the outlet. I turn and paddle back the same distance I had come along the shore, plus two more miles. Nothing. Beginning to feel lost, I head back to follow my first intuition. I chastise myself for not paddling to that chain of little islands before heading directly across. My arc screwed me up. But I'm sure I saw the chain of islands behind me. I'm sure I've landed south of the outlet. It must be the map's fault. Maybe I paddled too fast. Calm down, I tell myself. The narrows will show up.

I paddle into a small bay where I see a fifty-foot rock face, a mountain for this terrain. As *Loon* glides into the bay, a peregrine falcon streaks down from a ledge. In the stillness, it swoops over me. The wind sound made by its wings, the shrillness of its cry, startles me. In ever-widening circles the falcon climbs to watch. When the pounding in my chest subsides, I beach *Loon*, circle behind the rock face, and climb the slope to the top edge. I bring the camera in case there might be a nest. The peregrine hovers above me, too high up to look like anything but a dark spot. However, I am more interested in the view's relationship to the map. A part of me wishes I didn't care, but a larger part needs to locate myself.

From the top of the rock face I look south-southwest out the small bay to the large lake. Approaching the edge, I glance down its sheer face and there, twenty feet below, is a big nest. Around a center pocket is a tangle of twigs, sticks, and grass. In the pocket is an egg and two fuzzy white chicks. I forget about the map and smile. Flattening myself on the ground with my head over the edge, I watch. One chick is asleep; the other looks up at me. The adult peregrine whistles to its mate. They both hang like kites over the rock face. They have nothing to fear, but they don't know that I won't stay long. On the nest's rim are laid four small voles, each with its head pointed out and evenly spaced from its neighbor. Their orderly arrangement belies the impression that the peregrines are poor housekeepers. In fact, they're good housekeepers, and builders. Their home catches all the summer's sun, down to the last drop. My hand on the rock feels the warmth even though the sun has not been out long. The voles are the larder. The chicks are still too young to feed themselves. I take pictures of the nest, holding the camera shakily over the edge. Then I lay it beside me and return to watch, entranced by the peregrinette. An old nest lies in tatters beside this one. Have they moved next door, or is that the remains of another family's nest? Has this been a nesting site for generations, the way there have been hawks or falcons or both at Hawk Rapids since at least 1835? The little one below couldn't answer that. Its beak silently opens: feed me, feed me. Or is it saying leave me, leave me? In a few weeks, these young ones will be airborne, caring for their own needs.

The parents wheel overhead, awaiting my intrusion's outcome. How different from the mother ptarmigan who would throw herself at any threat to save her chicks. I feel I'm eavesdropping on something terribly intimate.

I've been anxious all day about my growing feeling of aloneness, and my desire to get back on the map. I am not sure what happened next, but suddenly, looking into the nest, my mind jumps an octave. My eyes see the nest, but my mind sees something more, as if it went behind the word "nest" to perceive a quality as fundamental as any element listed in the Periodic Table. The egg and two chicks, those sticks and the grass, the voles, melt away and shimmer in front of my perception. The silence around me changes from a vacant, passive one to a deep hum and begins to boil.

Rock merges with nest. The whole massive rock face becomes as much nest as the nest itself. This nest's circumference expands and expands to embrace the cliff face, the surrounding tundra where the parents hunt, where they will fly in the fall, and their journey back again. All is nest. The chicks are only the diamond edge of a circle stretching deep into time. Everything touches. The falcon holds its world in full confidence. As in the moment of transition that occurs in welding when solder, flux, and metal flare to give up separate identities, a strange heat envelops me. I pull away from the edge, roll on my back to watch the two windhovers watch me.

I begin to smile and breathe more fully. Then what I see begins to breathe me: the sky, the ground, even the rocks. We all seem to be moving slowly, as if we were about some construction work that involves the whole order of the universe and will take all time to complete.

Though temporarily lost, I've stumbled into a sense of time I've never felt before. I watch the falcons, their two dark shapes against a blue, blue sky, hovering, twisting off in the light breeze to circle lower or climb higher. They breathe me up to them in ever-widening circles, the way they gain height. The way a puppeteer lifts a puppet. They breathe me back down, but before they do, my mind slips loose and they show me their world. The higher we climb, the more the tundra spreads out, the lakes take shape, the rivers look like string. I feel the wind, the temperature, change. I see the loving indifference of their land.

I climb slowly down to *Loon*. The silence that has seemed dead white isn't empty anymore. Each birdcall or water noise is loud and pregnant with its own meaning. I glance about furtively as if someone I can't see is watching.

I get into *Loon* and start paddling. Leaving the bay, I glance back at the cliff face. On a day when I knew where I was, I wouldn't have stopped here. I don't know if I feel grateful, or terrified, for having been shown whatever I saw.

I looked for the outlet until I wore myself out. I had done it, really done it. I was lost. Or as Horace Kephart would say, I was "confused." If you're really lost, no one can help you. If you're only confused, then you can help yourself. I hoped so. I camped tucked in behind a wall of boulders on a point. I saw the whole lake. What I was looking for was a big island that sits off the shore of the mainland. If I found that, I would know I'd come too far and the outlet would be south of me. Tomorrow, I thought, I'll keep going until I prove I'm too far north, or I find the outlet. All this time images flashed back to me, of the land, the water, the rocks, and the nest. Each image rode a feeling. Each feeling was newly minted and shone in me.

III.

LOON

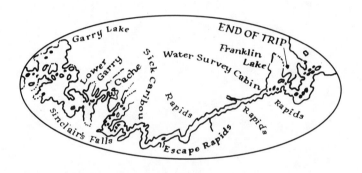

AUGUST 12–SEPTEMBER 3, 1987

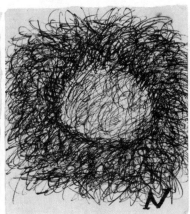

N *is for nest.*

To watch a nest is to eavesdrop on eternity. It is such a confident gesture in this world to build a nest. The world is our nest. We share the earth with a lot of other creatures, but it's like a nest. That's how we ought to treat it.

Today I'll see if I can find out where I am. I filmed my concern last night, saying, "You get security from three basic things: knowing who you are, where you are, and what you're doing. I've got two out of the three." Today I hope to solve the third.

Still believing the outlet is to the north, I paddle into a crosswind to prove it. Rounding a point puts me on a weather shore, where small waves wash past *Loon* to bump on the rocks to my right. The hunchback shape of a loon flies up from the south behind me, high up, and croaks its airborne cry. It circles around me and disappears back where it came from. I take it as a good omen, though it could just as well be a suggestion to turn around. There is a bay two miles ahead. I see an esker on the other side of it. I promise *Loon* that if I climb that esker and don't see the big island, or a hopeful sign of it, I will turn back. We'll retrace our steps, even across the lake for a fresh start if necessary. Although it is windy, the sun is out, warming what is otherwise a miserable day. On the far side of the bay, I duck out of the wind behind a bank. I leave *Loon* there while I walk to the esker, which takes an hour.

Each step on the esker sounds hollow. The view from the top reveals more indistinct shoreline and another severe expanse of lake. No big island. The waves run higher, kicking up white-caps. Something isn't right between myself, the map, and the land. The land can't be wrong. Although maps can be inaccurate and misleading, the problem is more often caused by the person who looks at them. Time to admit it: it must be me. I turn around and head south.

To retrace my steps will take a stiff paddle into a strong crosswind back to the point where I camped. Once past there, I'll run with the waves, taking advantage of the shore's nooks and crannies, but the first step is to cross this bay.

I head out to ferry sideways across the half-mile mouth of the bay, letting the wind edge me over as I angle into the waves. I aim to pass near, but not below, the upper edge of the bay. There my work will begin in earnest, paddling toward the point without letting the wind push me onto the rocks. Two-thirds of the way across the bay, my plan unhinges. Every third or fifth swell rises up higher than *Loon*. My paddling creates no momen-tum. I pray the big ones won't break until they pass by. I don't care about reaching the point anymore. I only want to get to land. The closest land is all rock. I stop and think. A big one catches me, sucking *Loon* into its trough, trying to turn the canoe parallel. The wave shatters into my lap. I grab the gunwales. Coming off the backside, we're still floating but half full of water. Sore from kneeling, I watch the wave recede, foam streaking off its crest.

I turn and run with the wind. Reckless, I angle toward shore. I want an opening, a point, anything to get to before I get hit again. Fifteen terrifying minutes later, there it is, not much, a comma shape of rocks sticking out. We turn the corner fast, *Loon* banking into it as a last wave slaps at us.

I jump into knee-deep water and tow a sodden *Loon* to shore. Wet and shaking, I am furious that I let my concern over where I was get ahead of what little common sense I possess. I never should have paddled in that junk. I almost paid the price. Just because the sun is out that doesn't mean I can't drown. I kick at a pile of caribou bones. Half a jawbone, polished white by the sun, looks like a bird carrying little teeth-people on its back. The scariest one is a caribou's upper skull attached to its antlers. I turn the skull to see underneath. I jump at what I reveal: a miniature human face, a demon face with round eyes and an open mouth, all bone.

From my higher vantage point I see the bay I tried to cross opens around in back of me. Off to the right there seems to be water, perhaps just a string of ponds, but I won't expose myself to those waves if I go to look. I apologize to *Loon* for what happened.

I paddle to the backwater I had seen behind the point to find myself out of the wind. In afternoon sun, families of ducks scurry from *Loon*. The land is green and lush. I don't know where I'll wind up, but I'm headed in the right direction. Every time my binoculars show a blockade of land ahead, the obstruction turns out to be islands. I thread between them. If I keep going I could be putting myself in position for a portage or a long paddle back the way I came. It's something to do, and so I go on . . . until an odd-shaped piece of the backwater's puzzle blocks my way. I beach *Loon* and climb its gentle rise. It's an island, with Garry Lake beyond! I hold the map to coincide with the direction I've been paddling, and this time, instead of telling the map what I want, I let it show me where I stand. In a minute, I have it. I stand six miles north of the outlet, on a small island next to the big island I am looking for. It's right there next to me. No wonder I couldn't find it last night: I was standing on it. Frazzled by my long lake crossing and seeing the peregrine nest, I missed seeing the gap between the mainland and the big island. I paddled right past it.

I feel dumb, but ecstatic. I'll camp right here. From the diminishing flour supply, I'll bake a bannock, adding some raisins to celebrate how stupid I am, and how lucky.

While I eat dinner, a "periscope creature" pays a visit—a ground squirrel. When they're not on all fours, mouth to the ground, selectively vacuuming the tundra for food, they're on their hind legs watching. Often they move their paws across each other like Uriah Heep, scheming to get more food out of life. Or they wind up as food themselves. I once saw a standing ground squirrel on a riverbank just as a jaeger swooped in to knock its head off.

The squirrels are a staple of their predators' diet, the biggest being the barren-ground grizzly. Bears don't bother with subtlety when they hunt squirrels. One arrives at a squirrel colony and simply begins digging, fast. Craters remain where they've scooped, pockmarking entire riverbanks. The bear's game is to toss up a few squirrels along with the rocks, dirt, and sand. The game for the squirrels is to have enough connecting tunnels to escape, or a massive rock on top of their last defense. If I were the squirrel family tactician, I'd have every child and able relative digging tunnels and forget about the rock defense. Photographs don't convey the amount of strength grizzly bears possess: what looks like thick fur on their forelegs is inches of solid muscle. Large rocks merely provide good exercise.

Another staple is the ptarmigan, more for raptors and smaller carnivores than for bears. The ptarmigan, whose nearest relative is the grouse, nests on the ground. To see one pass effortlessly over the tundra, its white wings locked in glide position, tilting only slightly to change direction, is to appreciate the story of Daedalus and Perdrix.

Daedalus was the great inventor who worked for Minos on Crete. To escape, he crafted wings for himself and his son. He could not stand rivals, especially if they were relatives. Perdrix, his nephew, was only four years old when he saw the spine of a fish on a beach and, turning it into metal, invented the saw. When he was six, he invented several navigation aids. His inventiveness did not please Daedalus. One day, when they were on a high tower, Daedalus pushed his nephew over the battlements. Minerva, the goddess who favored ingenuity, saw him fall and, to save Perdrix, turned him into the first partridge. This is why partridges, ptarmigan, and grouse never nest in trees; they stay close to the ground. All of which might have saved Perdrix from Daedalus, but not ptarmigan from predators.

The small island is covered with old campsites and stone meat caches. The ground is covered with mounds of discarded caribou bones so old, they've turned to wood. The longer I look, halted in my task of gathering firewood, the more I feel the presence of the land's former inhabitants. This is a perfect place to meet: it's protected, and in a short climb the surrounding countryside becomes visible. I finish collecting my sticks and twigs and return to make an evening fire. Hearing a haunting call rebound off the surface of the water, I remember the loon that flew around the canoe this morning. Like kindling for my soul, each time I listen to a loon's cry, I feel a warm reverberation.

For the first time in days, I relax. I'm over the worst part of the lakes. It's early August. I have almost three weeks to reach the end of the river. Tomorrow I'll head into Lower Garry Lake.

After filling my small coffeepot with water for the morning, I lie down to keep the fire company. The bugs aren't bad. I feed the fire twigs one at a time, watching the new wood catch and the old burn out. They retain their roundness as they turn to ash, whiter than the new bleached twigs I feed in. I get out my pipe, which I haven't smoked for weeks. Once lighted, the tiny hiss and pop in the pipe's bowl are miniature echoes of the larger noises in the fire. When both die out, I go to sleep.

I don't know for how long.

I'm thrown against the far side of the tent. I gasp for air and tear myself out of the dream.

I'm in a tree. The tree grows out of water. I can't see land. What I do see is my father in a small peapod-shaped boat, sculling away from me. I feel glad to see him up and about. Then I see he lies amidships on his side, legs dangling over the gunwales. He wears a hospital nightshirt, open down the back. He is too large for the boat. It swamps. I try to jump out of the tree. When I look again, the boat has sunk. My father lies in the water, floating on his back. His arms and legs are lifeless, slowly sinking out of sight. His head is still above water, but he makes no cry for help. His lips curl back.

I snap awake.

I lie there blinking, hoping to banish those strange images. My chest feels tight. I cry. There was nothing I could do—not even speak. The rest of my night is fitful tossing until I forget about sleep.

My thoughts I can evade, but not my dreams. Outside, everything is still. I make coffee, eat some bannock, pack up. I'm on the water before the sun rises, though the light curves ahead of me, tinting the far shore a pale-orange sherbet. I paddle over the flat, sleepy surface of the lake that yesterday almost killed me. Coasting through the narrows, I see other early risers: seven loons swim silently and dive and surface near the mouth of the narrows. Not to disturb them, I slide *Loon* close to the mainland shore. They take no notice of me as they pursue their breakfast.

I turn south, putting more force into my strokes. I head to the narrows separating the last Garry Lakes. I feel riled, but the quiet landscape acts as a counterweight gently tugging me away

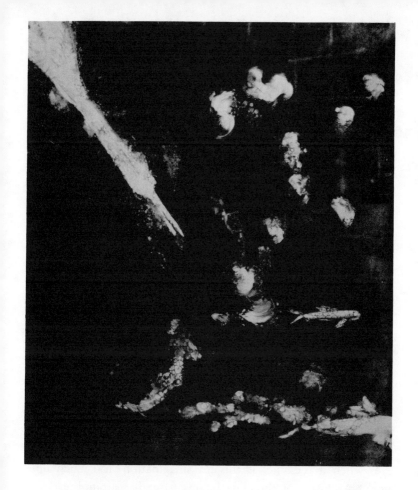

from the dream. A bumblebee passes near enough to hear, but not to see. I smile: I bet it flew over from the other side of the lake just to have breakfast. I look across at the barely visible horizon. What if I had waited and crossed today?

I reach the outlet in an hour and a half. Evidently the first evening I hadn't backtracked far enough south to realize my mistake. I turn into a maze of large and small islands, more "shreds." Paddling among them is a pleasure. Another hour and I stop to climb a hill to look at Lower Garry Lake. I can paddle to the lake's southern shore if I want another experience of open water, or I can make my way along the lake's north shore. Even with its numerous bays and longer mileage, the north side is my choice. I don't want to paddle over more open water.

The ground cover is grass and light-green moss. Nothing is higher than two inches, a uniform flat surface, a confetti-covered wedding street. The hillside catches the sun directly. Climbing it, I experience an odd sensation: for the first fifty yards, I sense the ground moving the way my eyes, if I stand up too fast, liquefy the landscape and white spots swim in them. Instead of white spots, these are dark ones.

I don't understand until I see the first black wolf spider, as thousands of others dart away to their holes. Above each hole is a transparent, bubble-shaped canopy of gossamer web. On sunny days, they must leave their dens for the warmth and like bored fishermen go for a stroll.

Carefully navigating from point to point, I begin my paddle along the north shore of Lower Garry Lake toward another narrows—one I don't want to misplace.

After a few hours, the feeling I had at the peregrine nest of being watched returns. I try to recall the cause but remember only the silence. I feel wary, like what I see in a wild animal's eyes when it sees me. Is this my imagination, too much time alone? A cluster of thoughts begins to gather around an idea. Since I paddle flat water, I let it have full sway, although my eyes continue to scan the land to my left, the water, and the point I paddle toward.

All summer I've been thrilled by the signs of the Inuit's vanished culture, the talismans of a wisdom able to inhabit the tundra without disrupting the harmony of its land and animals. The few marks they've made on the land are nothing compared to those we will leave in just one city block of New York, London, or Moscow.

Ever since I came upon the scraper, a sadness has diminished the thrill of discovery. The Inuit signs I see are the ruins of a civilization destroyed by my own. The same friend who said I "spend" my way down rivers also says how tired he is of hearing people complain that the old ways are gone. He says we should accept the present and go forward. I agree. Like Humpty Dumpty, all the government aid, land claim money, and museum staffs won't put the old culture together again.

Maybe I am being watched. Maybe there's one or two families of Inuit who didn't come in when the government called. They would have preferred their own slower, less comfortable, but proven, way of living. They might have kept themselves separate from those who felt inclined to trade with the missionary and the other whites. They would have seen the corruption in those who embraced the time-saving advances of this other culture, not to mention the effects of tobacco, flour, sugar, and liquor.

Knud Rasmussen tells a story of the Inuit camp near the mouth of the Back River:

> An old half-blind woman leaning on a stick came up to ask me for a sewing needle and thimble. "I have come out of my house to see a new person, a stranger, who is a grown man; I was born before all the others of my tribe, so the people I see are always newly born. My name is (the one who was made a woman). I am so old that I have nothing to pay with, and yet I am a woman and need both sewing needle and thimble. If you give me these things I can only repay you with a wish. And that is: may you live long! But if I were to add another wish to these words, a wish that comes from the experience that my age gives me, it is this: may you never be as old as I am."

Even if this group I imagine were able to remain aloof from the changes brought into the tundra by the white man, they would have had to show incredible restraint to resist assistance from relatives who slipped them needles, fishing line, hooks, and steel knives.

I would call them "People of the Wolverine"—because like the wolverine they would be wary, smart, and tough. Having seen what was happening to their relatives, they evaporated into the landscape, every few years moving farther from past hunting grounds, seeking seclusion.

It's possible to live in this immense area undetected, especially if no one is looking for you. There are no mining interests east of Beechey Lake. The few canoeists stay on the major rivers. In winter the noisy snowmobile announces itself, but there are few of those. The last Caribou Inuit families were taken off the land as recently as the 1950s. Maybe this other group vanished during the hardship years of the war. I like to imagine they are out here, never to be studied, not to be disturbed. Maybe that's who I feel watching me.

To check and recheck my position, I climb several hills during the afternoon. I don't want to get lost again. I sail ten miles on a gentle tailwind.

On long walks away from the river, I've come to realize the Inuit hardly felt restricted to the Great Fish, or any river, the way I do. To them, the whole tundra was one river. The food currents on this land-river are the migrations of the birds, the fish, and especially the caribou. The Inuit had to pay close attention to them, or starve. The land-river current flows perpendicular to the Back, its streams of energy grow out of the soil and flow into plants, into animals, and into the Inuit. They could not eat the grasses, but they could eat the caribou. They could not eat the insects, but they could eat the trout. At death they returned to the soil, the body became immortal: seeing others dead, eaten by everything from flies to wolves, they knew they would live on through other creatures. Even the lichens and grass found a home among their bones. They wrapped themselves in the skins of the animals they killed, made their houses from them, and turned every animal part into food, clothing, or tools. They transformed a sea of blood into a civilization.

This hydrology of energy flowing up out of the ground is what the Inuit had come to understand during their five thousand years here. They understood the concept of the nest as I had glimpsed it lying on top of the rock face.

I'm stuck with facts and struggle toward wholeness. Aspects of this land-river are taught in the West as separate disciplines, with little cross-fertilization. From kindergarten through college, I believed the world was a composite of separate items. The possibility that everything is already whole is not acceptable to our scientific minds.

My knowledge separates me from what's around me; each fact I know of botany or biology becomes a beam of light in a dark room, but the excitement in finding the scraper, or seeing the *inukshuks*, tells me that facts needn't be unconnected to the land or ethics. Around me everything remarks the whole.

The breeze freshens and I pull down my sail. Instead of pushing on, I camp. The land is rocky, full of thrusting slabs that resemble folded wet linen. These are the earth's bones, covered by a thin skin of soil. This is the Precambrian Shield. In the afternoon I see several groups of geese quietly waddle away from shore. Their gray backs blend so perfectly with the rocks, I wouldn't have known they were there if they hadn't moved. Climbing a hill to check my position, I see they are well into their molt from all the feathers scattered among the rocks. For dinner I wouldn't mind eating a goose, but I settle for split-pea soup. I lay out some Cream of Wheat for breakfast, fill my coffeepot, and go to sleep early.

B *is for* being, *and that's what I am, a human being.*

Responsibilities come along with that—ones I'm just now finding out about. The Inuit lived in circles and ovals. Things they knew about are still here: ptarmigan, caribou, fish, weather, willows, rocks, bugs. How they knew about these things now travels invisibly. It travels with their spirit as a conscience in the wind, with a shadow passport.

I dally an hour or two in the morning, to see if the strong tailwind abates. From any direction, a strong wind is no fun to paddle in. I start off hoping the wind will have died when I reach the narrows. Continuing along the north shore, I cross two wide bays and enter a maze of small flat islands. A strong following sea builds. I stay close to shore. Far ahead I see white dots moving fast. Is that a herd of white hares? All summer the hares have been shy. The dots become snow geese, avoiding me the quickest possible way. As they can't fly, their best protection is in the water or hiding on land, although among these gray rocks, they're hard to miss.

I set up my .22, a small-caliber rifle called an "Explorer Special." Paddling after another group of geese, I insert myself between them and the land. I keep them in the water where I have a better shot. An island appears to our right. As one body, they swim for it. I close the gap between us. Their whiteness makes an easy target, but trying to sight the rifle on a bobbing goose while I'm in a bobbing canoe isn't easy. On the third shot, one falls over and floats in the water. As if they had dropped something, the flock stops to look back at their companion before surging ahead. Only now do I see that some of them are chicks. On land the older geese hang back to let the younger ones catch up. I was able to come close because they refused to abandon the goslings. I paste over my guilt with the thought: that's nature's way. I pick up my goose. The others disappear into the rocks and willows of the island.

While I reorganize myself, three gulls pass overhead looking for scraps. Feeling smug that I had left them none, a few strokes later I glance back. They are diving at a gosling in the water. It must have fallen behind during the chase. I see red. Without even turning the canoe, I aim the reloaded .22 over my shoulder and empty its five shots at my rivals, the gulls. I put in the spare clip and paddle back to the scene of my crime where the gulls are trying to kill the young snow goose. While one gull swims beside the chick, the other two dart down from the sky. The small goose swims underwater—six yards at a breath. Up for air, the young snow goose pokes at the gulls who dive at it.

My arrival forces the gulls to back off. They fly to shore, land, and wait. Their arrogant assurance that the gosling will eventually be theirs makes me furious.

The snow goose treats me the way it treated the gulls, as

an enemy. How can I convey to it I want to help? I could let it head out into the lake, but there it would fall easy prey to the gulls. Or I could shepherd the gosling to shore, and see if it can find a safe haven until the other geese reappear. On land it may have a chance.

The gosling makes the choice for land on its own. *Loon* and I escort it in. Reaching shore, its thick little legs start churning. As I watch, a gull flaps down to walk with it, looking like an innocent escort until it leans over to grab the gosling by the neck. Three times it tries before I can get the gun loaded and splash out of *Loon* in pursuit. The little goose parries each thrust. I fire at the gull. Giving in to anger is unwise, but I am furious at the gulls, and at myself. I pull *Loon* onto a shore. With waves breaking behind me, she will fill with water and grind on the rocks, but I don't care. I run raving after the birds. The gulls change tactics, flapping far enough off to be out of range, yet close enough to watch.

I follow the small goose at a distance, hoping it will head wherever it feels safety lies. It leads us over the top of the island past a colony of old goose nests, where broken eggshells litter the ground. Finally, on the island's far side, it dives into a gully lined with willows.

I watch to see if it emerges. I wait half an hour. It doesn't appear. The hardest thing I've done all summer is turn my back on that gully not knowing if the gosling will survive. I walk past one waiting gull, too disappointed in myself to squeeze the trigger. After bailing *Loon* out, I head downwind, using my paddle to steer. The sun beats down, an accusing lidless eye boring hot into my neck.

That feeling of betrayal lingers. The wind coming over my shoulder bats the tie strings of my anorak. It rustles the feathers of the snow goose at my feet. Over my shoulder I watch the following waves.

In sixth grade I had a beautiful homeroom teacher. It was

ı her first year. She was blonde and attractively built, and her skin was a translucent, creamy white. Among her many appealing qualities was one of particular magnetic attraction to the boys in the class: she wore black bras. Not even our older sisters were that daring, and for the girls in our class it would be years before they could be half so advanced. We knew she wore them because her loose blouses created a demure V from her neck down to a point above her breast bone where a whisper of black peeked above the fabric. Her breasts were not large but our young eyes couldn't seem to drink in enough of this mixture of the revealed and the hidden.

We manufactured questions to get her help. Like a protecting angel, she would appear at our desks, lean over our young heads to instruct us, and at the same time reveal a fuller glimpse of her black bra, and that gently swelling valley between her breasts.

Not far into the year, a stranger, harder chemistry began to operate between her and a few of us. We had homeroom on the first floor of the main building. The big windows at the back of the class were three feet off the porch outside. For those sitting near them, a well-placed book, ruler, or pencil could be knocked off and retrieved only by going outside. The lucky one, or ones, had a chance to walk to the gym, or around the whole main building, with a return to the classroom timed to coincide with the end-of-period bell.

For months we continued these skirmishes. Our antics became more and more offensive. Our teacher's frustration, and her inability to control us, mounted. She often went for the headmaster, who would restore order, then hand the class back to her. One day she told the five worst boys to stay after school. Alone, we were like hydrochloric acid on a bright new penny.

She pleaded with us to reform. She confided that her job was at stake. She banged her soft hand on the desktop for emphasis. We weren't impressed. We threw spitballs and slammed our books on the floor. Soon several of us were standing on our chairs, openly challenging her.

One of us asked her if it was possible for a woman to give birth to a pig baby. Taken by surprise, she said of course not, whereupon he produced a copy of the *National Enquirer* with the headline "Woman Gives Birth to Pig Baby." Not knowing what to do, she started chasing him around the room to take it from him. A voice sounded in the room. We all froze. Someone had called her a four-letter word. He said it again. She stood in the middle of the room. We watched. We didn't even know what the word meant. She didn't know who said it. Eventually she let the newspaper fall to the floor. She walked out. The floorboards in the hall creaked as she disappeared.

Although we saw her again, we took no pleasure in it. Neither she nor any of us acknowledged that afternoon. Within one week she left the school.

The next day the sky is covered by clouds. Occasionally the sun slices through them to throw a beam of its light in irregular patterns on the landscape. I eat goose for breakfast, saving enough for lunch. By late afternoon I reach the narrows where the lake has cut an esker in half, creating, on either side of the narrows, a reflection of itself. I see mirages on the horizon, sparkling like fool's gold, contracting into nothing.

I climb the left half of the esker for a look ahead into Lower Garry Lake where my direction will change to northeast. This light wind will turn into an unhelpful crosswind over *Loon*'s left bow. I consider camping, but decide against it: as long as the weather is reasonable, I'll keep going.

Over the last few days, I've felt a change in the air. There is definitely an evening now. By midnight it's too dark to distinguish landmarks on shore. I want to get off these lakes. I want to feel the river's current running under *Loon*.

The motions of my days alone pass without comment. The sum total of my remarks are a fistful of poorly sung half-remembered lyrics and, other than my few minutes talking on camera, a few comments to *Loon*. If I happen to die here, I'll be eaten as I have eaten so much in my life. This thought no longer bothers me. My death would have as much consequence as a candle blowing out in the next room. I am a small enough flame standing on this esker.

On my first long canoe trip in 1970, which ended in Eastmain, Quebec, where I met the nuns, I got to know Nick Shields. He had come as a last-minute replacement. Everyone on the trip liked him. We became immediate friends.

If I had read Horace Kephart twice, Nick had too. If I knew a certain knot, he knew an equally good one. If the six of us were in a funk, he brought us out. At twenty, you just know your friends and he was a good one.

One particular evening stands out in my memory. The evening was a dull, quiet one with fog swallowing up the lake. The two of us had gone fishing. Nick was in the bow, but soon stopped paddling. He asked if I would continue quietly. I did. The fog seemed eerie to me, stealing all definition from the sky and the water, but Nick liked it. He said: "To have the courage to enter the unknown without an irrational reaching after fact with reason."

Later he explained that those lines from Keats had intrigued him, and he'd wanted to see if the fog would feel like the unknown.

Half a year later and a continent from Boston, he lay dead in a San Francisco street, shot five times in the back by a black militant with a Saturday night special—both of them victims of random social rage. Several days later at Nick's funeral, the five of us who had been his canoeing partners joined his family. That Nick was dead on a bright, warm April day didn't make sense. Outside the church I stared at a hundred red tulips, the reddest I had ever seen. I kept my resolve not to cry until later that afternoon, when I saw his growth records—dates marked in pencil on the front edge of his bedroom door. Now Nick knows about the unknown.

The current in the narrows dissipates in the next lake. Expecting a headwind, I veer left to angle into it. For the first half-mile it remains a tailwind, curving itself around the tall esker, reversing its direction. Farther from the narrows it swings into a headwind.

The August full moon shows through a chink in the slate-gray clouds. They cut its yellow roundness into a ragged horizontal strip. I settle on paddling to an island the map tells me is halfway down the lake. Near it is a point of land where I am to find the cache of supplies flown out by the film crew last month. To avoid being blown off course by the wind, I adjust my paddling to resemble a series of loose running stitches: north toward shore, angling off down the lake, then north toward the shore again. On the second series of stitches, I see muskox snuffling through the low alders.

For several hours I tack and turn, keeping my island destination in view. Tired as my arms feel, they keep moving, though my left elbow throbs. The wind tapers. For the remaining miles a light breeze scuffles across the water. As I near my goal, I see three islands, not one. I've overshot my mark, drawn past it by this cluster that is more than three-quarters of the way down the lake. It isn't dark, but it isn't light enough for the binoculars to pick out the island I missed behind me. From the top of one of the islands, I see the mainland beckoning. I see the point where my cache is. The more I think about it, the more I want to reach the cache tonight. The distance is manageable; if I do it, I'll be almost beyond these lakes. The light is brighter on the water than on land. Setting out, I convince myself, but not my arms, that this makes sense. Slowly my muscles warm up: there is no hurry. I have all night. I don't care where I land as long as it's somewhere on that point.

The light dims, shortening my sight. The shore I paddle

toward becomes a black line of separation between a dark sky and the water. The breeze wrinkles the light on the lake. The cloud of mosquitoes that accompanied me dwindles to a few that whine in erratic orbits around my head. I paddle, aware only of the water that holds me, my strokes, the sound of the paddle's shaft on the gunwale, my breathing. At some point I cross a no-man's land. I see something, not outside but inside.

I remember my home. We kids lived upstairs in a world of our own. The memory of that intimacy wraps something up in my life. I see the peregrine nest inside me and the nest of those years upstairs. *Loon* and I are being pulled forward toward a destination as unclear as the dark shrouded point ahead. For an instant the water becomes a field of wildflowers—bright spots of life and color. I can hear their stalks brush along her sides as *Loon* glides through them. As the image evaporates it connects with the lawn, the great American lawn, my mother dug up to make a field of wildflowers. Each spring for several years she plowed and planted, taking notes, while all was in bloom, to add more here, less there, until she created a garden painting of wild color and texture.

The landing spot on the point is smooth ground, and I skip the courtesy of unloading *Loon* before pulling her onto dry land. I grab the bow handle and drag her over a thin strip of sand onto the grass. I take only my tent and bedroll from the canoe. I put up the tent, throw my pack and myself inside. I zip up the mosquito net, unstuff my sleeping bag, and sink into a deep sleep. The cache has been out there this long, another night won't hurt it.

In my dream, an angry hand shakes my shoulder. Waking up, I find the wind rattling the tent. I've slept a long time. Outside, the weather is windy, gray, and cold. Poking my head out, I see I've pitched in the open. I look, but see no better place.

Time to scout for the cache, but before I do, I unload the

rest of *Loon*, turn her over, place a large rock on her bottom, and carry the wannigan to the tent.

I find the cache two hundred yards away, sitting on a rock. I see the spare paddle first. I know film is inside, but I am more eager to see what foodstuffs are there. I'm tired of what's left—except the Cream of Wheat. The weather grows mean, so before focusing on the box, I batten down the tent. For heavy wind, I use lengths of shock cord with hooks on their ends to connect the pegs in the ground with the loops on the tent fly—in a bad storm, lines tied directly from pegs to the tent grommets tend to either rip the tent or pull the peg from the ground. I'll need the shock cord today.

Feeling like a miser, I pull my treasure into my castle and open the cache. More Super-8 film. But wait: Here's a bag of Cream of Wheat! More raisins, brown sugar, more rice, more flour, and some Swiss Miss hot chocolate mix. I'd rather have the Swiss miss. No cheese—too bad. I make a large pot of Cream of Wheat with raisins then watch brown sugar melt on top of it. I savor every spoonful. The weather is raw and I crawl back into my sleeping bag. When I wake up it's snowing. The weather alternates between snow and sleet and I between snacking and sleeping. The next day is no better, unless more sleet is better than more snow.

The third morning, calm weather and a clearing sky arrive. I wake up with a ravaging case of the trots—too much Swiss Miss. Preferring the idea of traveling to sick immobility, I pack up. Around the point is a rapid leading out of Lower Garry Lake into Buliard Lake: I am anxious to move on. On the map the lake named after Father Buliard is the size of a thumbprint compared to the elephant prints of the Garry Lakes.

I paddle an hour before my stomach tells me to stop. On a bed of pink pincushions, a mosslike flower, I set the tent up near the tip of a narrow esker. By not eating much, and drinking tea, I begin to feel better. The sun and a blue sky help. I move slowly through my chores. Returning from a walk with no more than a handful of twigs, I build a small evening fire. As it dies out, I see my first weasel, thin as a pencil, carrying something in its mouth. As fast as I see it, it vanishes.

H is for habit. That's partly how I've made so much space - Rather, me in so much space. Home-like. Through habit. Repetition every day. Not exactly the same but close enough to establish familiarity and confidence. Routine. It's how Amundsen got to the South Pole.

viii. XXi. 87

H H H H H H H H H H
H H H H H H H H H H
H H H H H H H H H H H
H H H H H H H H
H H H H H H H H
H H H H H H H H H
H H H H H H H H H H
H H H H H H H H H
H H H H H H H H H H
H H H H H H H H H H
H H H H H H H H H H
H H H H H H H H
H H H H H H H

H

H *is for habit.*

That's how I've made so much space homelike. Through habit. Repetition every day. Not the same every day but close enough to establish familiarity and confidence. Routine. It's how Amundsen got to the South Pole and back, and Scott did not.

Crossing Buliard Lake, I set out knowing I have several miles of rapids ahead of me. A swift current runs between Buliard and the Upper MacDougall Lakes. Where the large lakes pare down to fit between two banks, the river bubbles up. Big eddy burps erupt and swirl in the current—fun to ride, but dangerous. If a contrary current catches my paddle, I could flip. I drift through them, the river's whirligig, twisted and turned at their will. All morning the river's pale slate color reflects the sky. At lunch ribbons of cerulean blue unfurl among the clouds, a hope of clearing.

I come to a bend and see a riffle. As I stand in *Loon* to scout it, it looks like a minor event in the life of a major river. We shoot it. From the bottom, looking back, it doesn't look bad, though it is definitely a rapid. Either I am ahead of myself— which I don't believe—or this rapid was left off the map. Over the summer I've noticed several rapids worthy of inclusion that weren't marked. That's not necessarily a bad thing; usually if it's not on the map, the rapid is runnable. Trusting maps can be a hazard, and these omissions keep me on my toes.

I imagine the annual meeting of the Maps Division in Ottawa, right before the Christmas party:

"Say, Halibut, let's put this rapid back on the map."

"All right, that's a good one. Been off the map ten years. Now, who's in favor of deleting two rapids on the Back River system, and marking one that doesn't exist onto the Korak, just to keep those canoeists on their toes?" Everyone agrees so they can get to the party.

I come to a second rapid not on the map. More curious than anxious, I treat it as a cartographer's oversight, not yet appreciating the morning current's swiftness and how many miles I have actually covered. This rapid is a long sloping curve to the left, then one up to the right: a broad U. For a second time entering a rapid without scouting, I turn *Loon*'s bow downstream, not even hugging the inside curve. In big rapids, I prefer doing a water-spider dance down the river's edge to going for the Vs. I stay as far from big water as possible.

I ride smoothly down the first side of the U. With no concept of what the bottom looks like, I merely steer, letting the current pull *Loon* toward the middle.

I laugh when I see the bottom of the rapid. It's big. The calm upper part deceived me. If I were on the inside curve close to shore, I could jump out in the shallows and drag *Loon* to safety, but not here. I think of my friend Beekman who made me promise to scout every rapid, wear my life jacket, and not take risks. Now here I am in a big rapid I've not scouted, without my life jacket, faced with two awkward choices: paddle against the current and the tilt of the river to reach shore, or head into the rapid's teeth and pray. I try the first option. Running in glass shoes on oil would be easier. Reluctantly I turn downstream, this time anxious. This is what Chris wanted me to film: "People won't believe how tough the rapids are, Rob, unless you show them."

Instinct tells me cut fast to the other shore, though it means going through several standing waves. The spray cover makes the difference between getting there and swamping. I run *Loon* onto a beach and get out to recover, shaking.

After a while, I look ahead, scouting this time. To finish the rapid doesn't appear hard. I could portage or shoot it. The second side of the U seems calm, even mild, compared to what I just came through. If I could cross the rapid at its end above the standing waves, I could run down the right shore to the bay below, vindicating myself. Sometimes in blackjack you double down on a pair of sixes, not knowing you're double stupid.

I set out. The river narrows before the final rush into the calm bay. I don't stop to consider where its force goes.

In most rapids I work too hard to get scared, but today I feel fear in my stomach even before I realize what the river is doing. As *Loon* swings into it, the river looks calm. Then, like the boom heard after a jet passes, my fear goes off. I see where the force goes: straight up. From shore, I could not see this solid hump of speeding water squeezed between the narrow banks. No time for reflection: Don't switch sides, just paddle! Then, off the hump's backside, I see the real danger: the back eddy. There isn't a knifeblade's thickness separating the downstream force of water from the eddy's upstream rush. Like the river's rude child, the back eddy spins *Loon* like a rattle, knocking us first one way then another. As suddenly it tosses us away. I throw my weight downstream, tipping *Loon* to the gunwale—if we had not hit the eddy's opposite force, we'd have tipped over. *Loon* takes in water as we heel the opposite way. I drop the paddle and hold both gunwales as *Loon*'s nose rams the bank. Safe; but it's a moment I won't boast about. Beekman would call me what I am, a fool. I'll quietly wrap this day up and consider myself lucky.

It is still early. I go on a long walk away from my camp and the river. I decide the rocks win first prize for what grows best here. I picture myself at the Yellowknife Fall Agricultural Festival staggering in with a record-breaking boulder, one I'd tended and watered all summer, to place it beside the prize-winning pumpkins, gourds, and squashes.

A short time later I find a relic, a true relic: a goose print embedded in a muskox turd. What makes this an important find are all the coincidences that created it: first, the muskox had to defecate; then the goose had to walk on it at the right time (too soon and the imprint wouldn't have lasted, to late and the turd would have been too dry to take an imprint); and third, I had to find it. This I will keep. Ten minutes in my oven to remove any remaining moisture, and I will proudly place it on the coffee table. Perhaps I can interest L. L. Bean in making copies. "Original reproduction goose print in muskox turd: price $62.50. For the outdoorsman who thinks he has everything."

Lying in bed, I pluck at the kalimba I brought for company. The other part of my mind reviews today's rapids. I had forgotten about the kalimba. Its sound has a smoothing effect on an otherwise lumpy day.

Next morning there is another headwind. Eager to reach Rock Rapid, I'm off early. Upper and Lower MacDougall Lakes are like the two halves of water wings, running north–south with a wide connecting channel between them. As I went to sleep last night, I realized what caused yesterday's bungle. The whole day I had relied on the map, not the river, to show me where I was. My fault was in not being *present*.

The morning headwind becomes a tailwind as I turn south after lunch. In Lower MacDougall storm squalls sweep across the lake, eager to keep moving. Rainbows turn on and off throughout the afternoon, like celestial roadsigns on the outskirts of heaven. Sometimes a dark receding cloud carries a fragment, or a squall has a small rainbow following behind it—while larger, full rainbows, sometimes three at a time, appear, as if to music.

Evening begins, and the wind drops. The clouds settle into large formations, and the sun, from time to time, appears with an unhurried warmth to light up various segments of the tundra. Several miles from Rock Rapid I stop to stretch my legs. I walk the length of a small island. Its hummocks are dry. What was a spring pond is now a garden of Arctic cotton. I near a heap of boulders at the far end as a stream of the sun's light reveals a congregation of white shapes. The dark-gray forms of jaeger bodies become visible—more than a hundred of them turn to watch me. Silence suits the jaegers. I hold my breath and take one more step. They lift off in groups of three and five, drifting away as a loosely woven fabric of sinister predators to fly out over the lake.

I camp on another island several miles farther where the lake narrows at the head of Rock Rapid. I pitch the tent behind a wall of Volkswagen-size rocks pushed up like so many grains of salt. Ice is an unending combination of forces: the twist of the earth from winter to spring; the lengthening days; sun that melts snow into the first trickles of water, a liquid key. In the river, the rising liquid pressure under the ice unlocks the tundra. As the snow continues to melt, from trickles to streams to a torrent of feeding rivers, the ice cracks: Overflow appears, evidence of the mounting pressure. For a week or ten days, the river rises. The ice becomes the water's chance to stack boulders into piles, slam icebergs into banks, run bergs up banks like plows, beaching them high, abandoning them to melt on their own, their furrows like dents in dough.

For me, on a quiet evening in mid-August, it's marvel enough to be in the presence of forces larger than myself. Camp in place, dinner eaten, I bring the kalimba and climb the rock pile to see the sunset. I pluck the kalimba's metal fingers. The clouds slow down, forming massive combinations. Their crusts and bottoms are purple gray, while outer fringes glow white. They crowd the sun, but the sun eludes them. The colors flatten out. Their definition disappears and they become one flat shape. I see no moon. As compensation, one tern appears, perfectly motionless, except for its wings. As it touches the horizon, the sun breaks out blood red, spilling its color carelessly on the water. By the time I climb down, the sky has darkened.

In the middle of the gray night, I half hear the wind rattling the tent. I roll over. Five minutes later the rain starts. A tremendous gust belts the tent. A pole buckles. The collapsed tent flaps violently, the loose fly lashes at me. I fumble inside. I have most of my clothes on, but still need my boots. Outside it's howling. The storm boils into camp from the southeast. So much for "red sky at night, sailor's delight"! I run to check *Loon*, leaving the tent snapping and banging. Although everything I have on is soaked, I dig out my raingear. I secure the tent. "What would Hemingway do?" I ask myself. "Why, he'd head for the nearest bistro and order a cognac." I laugh and set off carrying the soggy tent and wet bedroll. I have not picked the best island in the stream to camp on, but after what seems ages, I find a better spot, a slope the wind curves over. In my search for a clean, well-lighted place, I had passed nothing that wasn't either a rock field or under water. A dull gray light leaks into the sky, all the light I'll get, unless the sun also rises. The tent is unripped and the spare pole I carry will replace the broken one. My sleeping bag wrung out, I look for that cognac, but all I get is rain. It takes two trips to carry everything across the island to the new camp. The walking keeps me warm. The camera cases stretch my shoulder joints. Once resettled, I begin to cool off. I crawl into a wet sleeping bag and lie there wishing I still had a jigger of Glenfiddich. Instead I brew tea.

The storm blows hard for two days. Sheets of horizontal rain wash over everything. When the wind inhales, the rain falls straight. I stay in the tent. Diminished by the knoll above me, the wind's force lands on top, a sturdier area than the tent's side. I'm no longer wet, just damp. Between brewing cups of tea, I spend hours watching the weather, and grass blades. They have no choice about being in the rain. They are built for it, although I detect several that wince each time a fat drop falls on their head. Covered with tiny burred hairs pointing upward, the grass blades invite the water to stay, a slick coat. When my eye moves as close as it can to these droplets, they show me the world in miniature.

My thoughts drift to another mirror-coat, a man-made one of wishes that I saw near an Irish river southwest of Cork. Una and I had driven into the mountains to find the headwaters of the river Lee in a high valley called Gougane Barra. It was drizzling. Entering the valley and the mountains that surround Gougane Barra, the paved road ended at the top of a steep hill in a black oval pond of tar. A bored-looking pub sat to the left of where we parked. No one was visible. As we stepped off the tar into the rough wet grass, we entered a presence not from our time. The colors around us were deep green, ochre, and umber. The mountains farther away were a brooding blue, cut up and down with swaths of dark green. Mist floated in the valley. In cupped hands, the mountains held the headwaters of the river Lee.

Una saw the ruins of St. Finbarr's monastery first: the tiny cells, where the monks had confined themselves to live in silence, attested to a ferocious faith. Nearby I saw a tree, or what had been a tree. Twenty feet tall, with thick, broken branches reaching in different directions, it stood transformed into a strange, human thing. It had no bark left; it was covered in coins. From the lower branches to as high as people could reach, the tree was solidly studded with large Irish pennies. Each was tapped halfway into the wood, then bent to the side. They glistened in the mist, shining like the water droplets on the grass blades. Each penny reflected someone's wish, hope, or prayer. Una said they were left as offerings from the devout. I was awed by the thought but couldn't resist pointing out that the idea of killing a tree with coins to show devotion to a saint who didn't believe in money sounded typically Christian to me.

Made quiet by the conflux of mist, view, and tree, we drifted into the mountains. The higher we climbed, the more we felt enfolded by the presence of the mountain's spirit. I asked her to marry me. As soon as I spoke, I broke the spell. The mountains became merely mountains, far away and out of reach. For the first time that day, the sun appeared behind a fine skin of gray cloud. Like the woman in Balthus's famous painting of the mountain climb, Una stretched, turning toward the warm sun, holding clasped hands over her head, and said, "Maybe."

Now, looking out the tent through the rain at the river, back in my present, I hope Una is in hers. I brew another cup of tea and continue to watch.

During the remainder of the day, the wind and rain come in cycles slow enough for me to collect *Loon*. In the late afternoon I hear a loon croaking its flight call nearby. It flies upriver directly into the teeth of the wind. Six gulls chase it. They resemble cloth towels flapping in the wind; every several yards one of them gets knocked back by a strong buffet, but they don't give up. To encourage my team, I cheer on the loon at the top of my voice.

L *is for loon*.

Handsome bird: black and white, but not read all over, just its eye. It is the wisdom of its colors, eternal yin and yang with an Egyptian profile. A hunchback in flight, the Quasimodo of the North. I saw one today chased by six gulls. The loon escaped.

The storm moves on. The gray clouds remain. Leaving my island camp, I approach Rock Rapid on the left side. I find the ledges and standing waves too large for my *Loon*. As I hardly want to paddle upstream and cross over for another look, I will have to portage. The tent and my clothes are soaked. I hate being wet, but I'll have to wait for a sunny day to dry out. The rock's appearance is hardened by the rain, and today's gray sky contributes a brooding aspect.

I carry the lightest pack first, to check the route along the skirt of this small mountain. Every rock is slick but any other place I put my foot squishes in response. The climb down the back side is steep, but there's a beach beside the big eddy at the rapid's bottom. Inland and up a hill, I am surprised to see a cave and a large red rock the size of a small house, its rusty color sets it apart. I stand beside it and ham for my camera like Hemingway with an upside-down trophy marlin.

I return around the rock's other side to see if the walking is easier. Part of the way back overlooks an ancient, dry streambed. Perhaps in spring the streambed fills, but now it is a rabble of gray stones. From the downstream side a falcon sweeps low over the dry bed. It banks right toward the face of the ravine on the far side of the empty streambed. Its landing on a ledge initiates small frantic cries.

I bring the canoe over the portage last. Near the end, my left foot slips from a rock and *Loon* flies off my head. My ankle turns and I feel something pop. I crumple fast, a puppet whose string is cut. In agony as I cradle my foot, at last the bone pops back. I tentatively get up and put weight on it. I can walk, but barely. I decide on an early lunch, catch a trout and boil it. I smile to think I'd be ready to enter the roundtable argument on char with Eric Morse at the Redeau Club.

The second phase of Rock Rapid is runnable. By late afternoon I'm back on the river, glad there are no more large lakes. I come to an island with rapids marked on either side. I choose the left. *Loon* glides over black water to land. Scouting shows me I don't want to shoot these rapids. It would be cumbersome to walk and reload after a quarter mile, only to unload and portage a few hundred yards farther. I decide walking is what my sore ankle needs and set off with the light pack. The land is flat— mile after mile of uniform ground cover rolls away, with no visible sign of life, creating the illusion of flatness. The thicker lines of green indicate alders and water, perhaps a stream. The conclusion of a sandy knoll's curving line shows how a ridge cuts it short; a gully.

That's the land. The sky is the tundra's partner. We have a shadow, the tundra has the sky. The sky is the other half of what draws my eye to the rim of the horizon, the rim of the cup I drink from today. In the storm's breakup, the clouds seem like big American cars, Lincolns and Cadillacs, heavy and powerful, cruising through heaven while their shadows race across the earth.

My ankle feels better; it's not going to stop me. The portage takes me across streams, over a mosaic of tussock colonies, through mushy fields of Arctic cotton balanced by the sandier beds of lupines in bloom. At the crest of a sloping piece of riverbank, I find medium-size stones tapped into the soft ground like the cobblestones of an ancient city street.

When I can see where the river rejoins itself at the bottom of the island, I locate a level place to load *Loon*. I drop my pack to mark my campsite. On the walk back, an owl lifts out of a bush, startling me. I go there to see what it was up to, but there's nothing to tell me. During the next several hours of portaging, the sun comes out. I meander, drawn here and there by something to look at, absentmindedness, or the hope of an easier walking surface. Sometimes, when I come upon my own footsteps, I believe there's someone else here. My eye spots a gray steel tent stake sticking out of the ground. When I pull it out, it is thirty inches long, a winter stake. The pegs I use are six inches long. I reset it, hammering it below the surface with a rock. Whoever they were, they had a beautiful view.

The river below me rumbles a greeting to itself as each half spills through separate rapids to meet the other at the end of the island. Downstream looks like a fast current. I'll make good miles tomorrow. Laid in the sun, my clothes and sleeping bag are almost dry. I've been traveling now for fifty-eight days. That gives me two more weeks to reach Franklin Lake and my rendezvous with Chris and Denny. I'll celebrate and cook the last popcorn. As I eat it, ready for bed, I read about Captain Back's arrival at Sinclair Falls, where I hope to be in a day or two:

It was in one of those singular and dangerous spots, which partake of the triple character of a fall, rapid, and eddy in the short space of a few yards, that the crew owed their safety solely to an unintentional disobedience of the steersman's directions. . . . The steersman was endeavouring to clear a fall and some sunken rocks on the left, but the man to whom he spoke misunderstood him, and did exactly the reverse; . . .

. . . At the awful moment of suspense, when one of the crew with less nerve than his companions began to cry aloud to Heaven for aid, McKay, in a still louder voice, exclaimed, "Is this a time for praying? Pull your starboard oar." "Heaven helps those who help themselves" seems to have been the creed of the stouthearted highlander.

The next morning the river current carries me quickly to the falls. I hear them long before I see them. Careful to keep my distance, staying close to the right shore, I creep forward. A light granite core of massive sculpted rocks extends across the river, forming the lip of the falls. The spacing and crowding of these rocks is the work of a master's hand. I've gotten out to walk among them. I'm a long way from the falls, but the shorter portage is over these works of wonder. I start across the top of the river's U; the bottom of the U is the falls. I walk up the back of these giant boulders, jump from one to another. I take my time, test my weak ankle, pleased that what I imagined as an arduous day is turning playful. At the end of the carry, I take time to sit and look, noting unhappily that the black flies are returning.

I sit on a flat rock above the river, feet dangling, my heels knocking lightly. Behind me is the center of the heavy rapids and the falls, but I'm enchanted by a small sideshow. In front of the point's lead rock the current circles gently by small rocks to flow over a miniature shoal. At the shoal's edge, half the water runs over a shallow rapid. These ripples, tiny as minnows, become lines of sunlight that project wobbling lines of light onto the darker rocks of the point behind.

Back in the canoe, as I paddle in a swift current, the sound of the falls lessens with each bend of the river. When I no longer hear it, I camp. That heavy a water sound makes me nervous.

Jostled gently out of sleep, I first wonder where I am. Still sleepy, I remember I dreamed I met my great-great-grandfather, the sea captain from the photograph. He stood on the rim of a pond, a city pond, above his reflection in the water. In his hands he held a model of a clipper ship. There were many people around him, but no one paid attention to him. Halfway around the pond, I saw him beckoning. Other boys sailed model boats on the pond, but none like his. She was beautiful, her topsides a deep blue. I took her and she felt light in my hands. Her lines were graceful, her whole aspect handsome. She looked as if she could sail on forever. I turned her in my hands to see her name: *Time*.

The last storm has shaken the flowers. Many have gone. The remaining ones look battered. Yet as I take down the tent I notice several Arctic poppies, bright spots of pure, condensed sunlight in a cool morning. Two bowls of Cream of Wheat should last me into the afternoon. I have one—if not two—day's paddle to reach Escape Rapids, about a week from the end of the trip. The Back River could be paddled in at least half the time I'm taking, but I hate to rush.

In the afternoon fat gray clouds invade the blue sky. Gliding over the water and landscape, their mottled shadows, alternately dimming and spotlighting the water, blend what I see with my imagination, enough to make me unsure of whether it's a caribou swimming the river ahead or not. Neither binoculars nor squinting helps. The river is broad, at least half a mile wide. I nudge *Loon* toward the shape. It is a caribou, but instead of swimming, it seems to be lying on the water. Then I see the sand bar spiraling out from the shore.

The caribou's legs are tucked under its body. Its head stretches out on the sand. It isn't moving, and it shows no interest in me. Maybe it's stuck in the soft sand and can't get up. *Loon* drifts to a stop twenty feet away. The caribou shows no sign of fear. I get out. Looking in its eye, I feel something familiar even though we look at each other over a gap of incomprehension. It's the look of an animal in a zoo: no focus, no interest. It isn't stuck; it must be lame. I move closer. Not until I am five feet away does it stand to trot ten feet farther off. It's a male. There is nothing wrong with his legs. He moves gracefully. I turn to walk back to *Loon*, then stop as a chill runs over me: he's sick. This sand bar is his last defensive position to watch for wolves, or whatever else might approach. Unless he can cure himself, this land will feel him die. His eyes will disappear first.

As I paddle away, the caribou returns to his post. The sun has come from behind one of those fat, gray clouds, turning the water surrounding the caribou into sparkling minnows of light. The last time I look back the cloud's shadow play of light and dark on the water has absorbed him.

Z *is for zoo.*

Today I saw a sick caribou whose eyes had the look of zoo animals, glazed and unfocused. Wild animals left the center of our lives a long time ago. Are zoos the way to bring them back? To get a baby muskox for a zoo, they used to have to shoot the protective mothers. Now they tranquilize the mother first, or bring her along. Big improvement. Someday people will look back at zoos the way we now look back at the practice of hanging witches. It may help educate people to look at animals in zoos, but it doesn't help the animals in them.

It took three days for the chill of seeing the sick caribou to leave. Last night not even the kalimba helped. But I uncovered something here that does: a love affair between the wind and the sand. They incline toward the smooth, the round, and the soft. All afternoon, paddling by one long esker, I see the wind through what it has touched. It molds and caresses the pliable sand, kisses its humps and gullies, its thighs and stomach. The wind is a tongue, an eye, a hand, a weight. Wind is an insatiable, fickle lover running to another surface, but always coming back. This love affair has lasted millions of years. What would it be like to be the wind and caress the large open plane of a buttock, to swoop to the nubbin of a toe, to nibble the tender spot above a sand elbow? Sand guides the wind. Neither abandons itself to the other; their trying to come closer would become a continual falling apart. Today I see them at rest, but a blush lingers in the esker's shape.

Ten days before my rendezvous with the plane, that should be ample time. I'll meet Chris and Denny on Franklin Lake near where the river leaves the lake on its way to the Arctic Ocean. We'll have three days to cover the trip's last ten miles so that Chris can complement what camera work I've done with his filming.

The river is growing in size, in power. I can no longer paddle close to both banks. At night, it's now dark enough to see the planets. I saw Venus and a young moon last night. I also saw a hare: not its body; just the white insides of its ears and the back feet, aglow in pale moonlight.

Fall is coming. Some leaves among the ground cover show hints of red and yellow. Berries are ripe. This morning forty snow geese took off in a white explosion, each bird a separate, animate piece of airborne confetti. I haven't seen these signs of fall's arrival all at once, but their sum, and the constant tickle of cold weather, says it is nearby.

It's impressive how seeds get themselves around. At lunch I see a bear scat full of leaves and berry seeds. In the evolution-of-design category, the seed offers itself in an attractive package, colorful and sweet. The packaging is removed by the digestive juices of the animal or bird that eats it, as payment for carrying the seed. Tough enough to withstand the juices, it waits inside the animal or bird to be dropped into a new range, complete with fertilizer.

My diet is now lean. No more frills like raisins and brown sugar with my Cream of Wheat. No more coffee, just tea. Even hot water is gaining popularity. My fuel should last, but if not, there are always twigs, and plenty of fish.

With the air temperature dropping, the thought of falling in the water scares me. They say you've got about ten minutes before hypothermia sets in. The water temperature hovers around thirty-eight degrees. Falling in when the sun's out is all right, but when the air is almost as cold as the water, it's deadly. From what I read, hypothermia is not an unpleasant death: everything in your body slows down, your will evaporates, and toward the end you lose consciousness. Wearing my skindiver's vest as an under-shirt gives me an extra three minutes. I'm happy to have it.

When I reach Escape Rapids, the wind is too strong to travel farther so I camp. They say a trip does not begin until you're hungry. Well, I'm hungry. The way a wolf watches geese, I watch the vapor trail of a jetliner flow across the blue vault of heaven. The wolf may not know what a jetliner is, but I do. Over the summer I've seen a few, but then I wasn't hungry. I lie on my back, hands behind my head, and dream myself into a seat on that plane: a stewardess passes down the aisle asking what we would like for dinner.

"To start, I'd like some shrimp—say, fifty medium-size ones. Then some hot potato soup followed by half a dozen ears of fresh corn. Don't melt the butter, I like a big slice on my plate to twirl the corn through. For an entree, I'd like broiled swordfish, two inches thick. I'll have a bottle of muscadet. Have you got all that?"

Before she answers, I continue:

"I forgot dessert: angel food cake with strawberry sauce on the side. I'll compress half of it, like I did as a kid, and put it in my pocket for later. You'd be amazed at how small a piece of angel food cake can become."

The stewardess interrupts me to say she does not have those things; she's sorry. When she turns around I return to the river, watching the last glimmer of the silver fuselage wink its good-bye. I get up, dust the sand off my pants, and return to my tent to fix rice.

In the early hours I wake up. Something has bumped the tent's guy line. I lie still but don't hear anything. I feel a tug on the guy line from the opposite side. Whatever it is, it's big, not a ptarmigan. The next time the whole tent shakes.

I sit bolt upright; it's a bear.

I have two options: play dead or make noise. I'm not going to play dead until I *am* dead. My mouth opens to bellow out "For All the Saints, Who from Their Labors Rest." I hold an M-80 firecracker in one hand, the lighter in the other. An M-80 is the equivalent of a quarter stick of dynamite—there won't be much left of the tent, or me, if I light it inside.

All is quiet.

I unzip the mosquito netting and reluctantly poke my head outside. It is a grizzly. The bear stops on a rise twenty yards away to look back at what must have been a rude shock. It grunts and runs off.

I could be glib and say my singing scared it, but the bear was only three feet away with every advantage. I was dumb lucky, that's all. The bear didn't appreciate its opportunity; the tent would have been easier to open than an oyster.

When I try to sleep again, either my eyes pop open or I sit up every few minutes, stories of maulings fill my head.

G _is for grizzly._

Barren-ground grizzly bear, _Bruno kindaferocious tavernacious._ It doesn't need a calling card; it is one. A beautiful creature, but one to keep at a distance. The best defense, if one comes nosing around your bed, Marshall, is to pretend you're an oyster, and sing.

Over the next few days, the water running from Sandhill Rapids to Wolf Rapids is tough. I shoot a rapid, walk around another, shoot a section, walk again. Trying to weasel my way past rocks, or ledges, I'm forced offshore to run rapids in the middle. My ankle remains sore. The riverbanks are steep, making what was painful walking on a flat surface excruciating on a slanted one. And it's not only my ankle that hurts: the balls of my feet and big toes are rubbed numb. I do what I can at night to revive feeling in them, knowing they'll be as bad the next day. My right hand now is stronger, but the muscles have thickened and it won't form a fist.

A cold front moves in. I wear everything at night, and I'm still cold. This is the price I pay for bringing a summer-weight sleeping bag. At least the black flies are gone. Lichens, the flowers of fall, spread in muted tapestries on the rocks and reclaim my full attention after the summer flowers' departure. The silence is heightened, like that in a hemlock forest, in a windless snowfall. At night it burns into me. The slightest rustle becomes another bear. For comfort, I pluck at the kalimba. Its notes weave their own silence: between them lives a catch-breath, a quiet between the facts. I am aware of myself ticking, alive.

On a point that is an isosceles triangle studded with rocks coming into the river from the right, I see snow geese feeding at its tip while a white wolf stalks them. What sun there is comes over my shoulder and keeps me invisible but illuminates what is pains-takingly unfolding. Some geese are in the water, most are on shore, milling around, unaware of the wolf. They won't see it until the wolf stands. I barely twitch my paddle to keep *Loon* positioned. The wolf reflects the shape of the point, high in the rear, low in front, its butt lifted just enough to let the back feet move it forward. Infinitely slowly, its focus on the geese a lover's intensity, the wolf reaches the critical point and leaves the shel-tered area. It moves even more slowly, like a wind-up toy at the end of its wind.

It springs, and the geese cry out. Each one leaps into the air or the water.

The wolf stands, astonished that they all escaped. Its tail hanging, it trots back along the point.

I'm luckier and catch two trout for dinner.

The next morning the weather is crisp. All summer I have come closer to seeing my place in the whole and the whole as it is. I watch what is around me with an ease and acceptance I've never felt before. I remember an Irish myth about a son who goes on a quest for an elixir to cure his dying father. He finds it. I wonder if I haven't found it too: understanding. But it is more for me than for my father. Now I understand the journey he's on and know that I'm on my own journey.

His crowded mantelpiece, his clocks and boat, are his symbols of order in chaos. The peregrine's nest gave me mine. What counts is that we have put in order what matters most. I only hope I get home in time to show him that I understand.

A chevron of black and gray geese flies into a stiff wind. They reflect the contour of the land, like shadows. I see three snow geese mixed in with nine Canadas: three white pearls on a string of black ones. I see a small flock of martlets heading south.

Last night's frost sparkled in the sun for an hour this morning. What started as a bright fall day is being eaten up by gray cloud. The river is wide and majestic, presenting corridors ten miles long to the next bend. Pretty as these views are, especially passing Mount Meadowbank, I don't like them. Paddling mile after mile over open water creates the feeling that I'll never get there. Any strong wind will force me to stop.

I let *Loon* loose in the current while I relax. She drifts toward shore. I pick up the paddle, about to stroke, as a loon streaks out from the rocks straight at me. Steamrolling to get airborne, it doesn't see me. I duck. The loon veers. At that close a range I saw how it carries its feet, touching as hands do in prayer.

A large white wolf stands on the shore, the reason for the loon's hasty departure. I see a second, larger, white wolf. Watching them lope directly away from me is like watching something only half there. The small ration of sun brightens one side, their white fur makes their shadow side invisible. They look flat, like cutouts.

By evening I've gone through several rapids. The full sun

returns. There's no wind. At the next bend I put into shore to look for a campsite. Just over a rise I see a cabin. That's not unusual, but when I see someone come out of it, I drop behind a rock. Two men work, doing carpentry, building something. I'm only a few days from the end of my trip, but if the idea of bypassing the cabin enters my head, I quickly put it aside.

The cabin sits above the river in a small notch in the shoreline. I return to *Loon* and paddle in, beach her, and approach. Both men are in the cabin. I hear a power saw.

"Hello." The gasoline generator drowns me out.

"Need a hand?" I say louder.

The noise stops, the door whips open, and a head pops out. The man looks surprised. We watch each other. He walks out the cabin door, followed by another man.

"Hello. I'm Derek," says the older man, offering his hand. "This is Henry."

I can't stop smiling. "Hello. I'm Robert."

They invite me to have dinner. They work for the Water Survey, studying rivers. Their plane will come in the morning and they need to finish up, but they won't let me help.

Derek hands me a cold beer. I like the taste of it. I watch them work. At dinner they tell me news of the world. I have a difficult time talking about my trip.

The heat in the cabin, the food, and a few more beers force me to bed early. In the tent, falling asleep, I compare the world's tragic news to what I've experienced: men die miserably, every day, from lack of what I have found here.

Their plane comes early. Derek invites me to use the cabin if I wish. I stay a day to relax, clean pots, and get ready to end my trip.

I go blueberry picking, a quiet task except for the *plink* of a berry hitting the bottom of the pot. I see how thick my fingers have become from paddling and lifting.

I think of Captain Back. Although he didn't map any new coastline, he discovered this inland waterway to the Arctic Ocean. He didn't lose a man. Back's journal became a standard work in the libraries of ships headed into the Arctic, providing a blueprint to safety from barren coast to the interior. When Sir John Franklin set out to discover the Northwest Passage in 1845, an edition of Back's journal went with him.

I thought of Franklin's 105 men, stranded on King William Island, north of Chantrey Inlet and the mouth of the Back River. For them the Back was their passage to safety. Men too weak to continue were made as comfortable as possible. Each small group left behind was promised that help would come as soon as they found it. None of them survived.

I make blueberry pancakes. I'm in a house. I have light, heat, furniture, bedding, tools. Amazing.

I sweep the floor, just for the pleasure of it, several times. I even try to dance with the broom.

I work on a Tundrabet, more for me than for Marshall, but how would you illustrate it?

C is for Culprit. I know a woman who loves the planet. Her scrutiny of history has turned up the biggest culprit: man. He's done more to ravage the earth and slaughter its creatures than any other species. There isn't a close second. If you love people, she says, this might seem defensible. If you love the planet, it's not. Western societies have done the most to push the hands of the clock toward midnight, especially in the last three hundred years, but the eastern countries are not far behind.

I never say anything when Elizabeth talks about this. She's right, but it's impossible not to be human. As we're human, she says we could exercise restraint. We could care for our fellow creatures. Civilization is an experiment that has failed; only technology keeps it limping along. Slaves to false needs, we blind ourselves to the destruction we cause. The equation for survival is simple: the more people there are, the greater their needs, the greater their demand on the planet's resources. We have to cut back on births.

In one of her history books she relates the story of the Spanish Armada's arrival in Mexico, off the peninsula of Tabasco. The natives couldn't see the Spanish ships, although they were anchored in sight of land. Whatever they thought them to be— clouds, mirages, fabulous gods—they had no concept of what they represented to their civilization. If they had known that in a few years their civilization would lie in ruins, that they would become Spanish slaves, they would never have let the Spanish land.

I often ask my friend what the Armada of our day is, what we can't perceive because we have no concept of it. She never gives a direct answer, but reminds me that the choice is this: are you for people, or for the planet?

At the start of the next day the river is swift. I watch the shore and rocks whiz by as if they were moving, not *Loon*. I think about Captain Back and his time's commitment to discovery and progress. I think about Elizabeth and ask myself if her conclusion is mine. Am I for people, or the planet? The rocks, the water stream by—answers seem less relevant than questions. Individuals are the basic building blocks for change, not institutions. I am for whoever and whatever respects the earth. You might call me a Blue Domer—the blue vault of heaven is the roof of my house, big enough for anybody.

Two days later I approach an island. I head toward the left side, the thinner of two channels, only to find it empty of water. I beach *Loon* in the muck, too excited to paddle to the small island's other side. The last tough rapid on the river. I hop on the visible rocks dotting the shallow water, bearing in mind what Captain Back wrote about Whirlpool Rapids.

> From its giddy height the rapid looked as even and smooth as oil; and in that supposition, having taken the precaution to lighten the boat forward, we pushed off, and the next minute were in it. I think I shall never forget the moment of the first descent down what cannot be more fitly described than as a steep hill. There was not, it is true, a single break in the smoothness of the surface; but with such wild swiftness were we borne along, that it required our extremest efforts, the very tug of life, to keep the boat clear of the gigantic waves below: and we succeeded at last only to be tossed about in the Charybdis of its almost irresistible whirlpools.

Ringed by rocks, the island isn't big. Scampering over its center, I sink into spongy moss hummocks. I can hear by the roar that the other channel has plenty of water. On the opposite side I see one beautiful sheet of black water curling over a rock shelf. At the bottom, on the left, are standing waves. If I stay to the right, there's an avenue wide enough to paddle pinwheels through! *Loon* will be as pleased as I am. The water must have been stronger and high when Back went through. What I see is a piece of cake. After returning to *Loon*, I back out, paddle around, and shoot the rapid. We drift in the fast water below, *Loon* doing slow circles while I look wherever she points. Smiling, I think of all that lies behind us.

The rest of the day is open water. While Franklin Lake's shores stay close together, I watch their dips and curves, their sandy places and the leafier green folds of the streambeds. Eventually the west shore meanders away on a course I'll never follow. I stay on the east shore. The pearl-gray sky is seamless, the surface of the water is the color of ink. Somewhere down the lake, the soft, muffled conditions accelerate the cry of a loon. Its rapid calls pile up on one another, not waiting for the last to fade before the next begins.

The sound stops. It starts to snow, and I wonder if the loon's cries were heralding it. Flakes landing on the spray cover sound like sprinkled salt. I see a collection of intricate, miniature butterfly snowflakes pinned on the hairs of my anorak. The snow hitting the water makes no sound, leaves no trace, as it dissolves. I camp and get out the camera to talk about finishing the trip. I try out one of my firecrackers to see if it actually works. It does.

Before sleep, I go on a brief cold walk. The only thing moving in the landscape is a pair of sandhill cranes. I have not seen these birds all summer. These two are staying late in the north. To see their backs covered with snow is like watching Ovid finish one of his stories of metamorphosis. I wonder what his moral would be.

Entering a small streambed, I imagine myself a walking minnow. I move toward hills far from me. When they appear no closer, I shrug and turn around. It's still snowing. Not far from the streambed, I see a bone, white among a ruckus of green and brown: a piece of my future, outside my body.

I've lived a cycle here, run its course through spring to the beginning of winter. The next morning I watch the tall grasses, the juice sucked out of them by the cold, turned to pale straw. I hear nuances I hardly dreamed existed. I see more of what has always been here. I see with my whole body, with a far less frantic eye.

I paddle past one or two islands without enough cover to block the wind. The sky is still gray. The snow has stopped. It's cold. Five miles shy of the lake's outlet, and a hundred yards offshore,

I find a good island with a cliff face where I can tuck into the rocks, protected from the north wind. I can use the small plateau on top to signal the plane. For the last time I make camp on my own.

The plane will bring Denny and Chris to travel with me the last three days of the trip. With them will come the tether returning me to my kind and news of my father. I dread hearing he's dead—or that he is a bedridden husk.

The river, the loons, the rocks, the wind, the wolves, the fish, the birds—even the black flies have played their part, wedging their way into my thoughts and dreams. All those eyes. How many I felt but did not see; they all seemed to say:

"If you love us—really love us—don't come back."

The island is made of dark-gray granite covered with light-green and black lichen. Where the rocks allow it, patches of moss and grass grow. My tent is pitched comfortably on one of these patches of thick grass. On top of the island, above the small cliff, I lay out my yellow tarp to attract the plane. Climbing down from the top, I find an old falcon nest, complete with bones, droppings, and a heap of sticks reorganized by the wind.

After the second night, the plane still hasn't arrived. The tent rattles. The wind shifts, sweeping in from the east. The snow sounds like a thousand needles breaking on the fabric. Of all the recent nights that I regret having a light sleeping bag, this is the worst.

Cold and tired, in the morning I unzip the tent door. The storm has left in its wake a landscape transformed. The snowcover whitens the dark rocks and makes the gray day seem bright. The lake remains jet black. The only color is the wannigan's red. It reminds me of an eye.

When I decide it's colder in bed than outside, I get up, brew tea, and begin the long wait.

Unknown to me, Denny and Chris encountered delays. The company flying them was moving char in from the fish camps. They waited two days. They said their friend had been traveling alone for seventy-two days. The pilot snapped, "The fish will spoil; your friend won't."

When the plane was available, the blizzard hit, holding them back another day. Denny described how after the storm, the clouds were gray, but soft. They sat stuffed between slimy, wooden crates of char. The flight from Gjoa Haven, where they had picked up the fish, revealed a black ocean meeting a white land. An equally black ribbon of river flowed north between white banks. Reaching Franklin Lake, they began to look for me along the east shore. They thought they saw me a dozen times. Then I was spotted a mile ahead. The island was round, Denny said, a large plum pudding on a shiny black tray. My running back and forth in the purple anorak attracted their attention, he said, like the purple flame on top of the pudding.

To me, while I wait for them that last day, every noise is the plane. Every thought that strays circles back to the plane. Even sounds that don't exist draw my attention to look for the plane. Finally, yes? No. Yes! There it is, a black peppercorn, flying low on the horizon, working its way toward me.

Neither the plane's arrival nor Denny's whoops mingling with mine compares with the shock of the two words he says when he quiets down.

"He survived."

Into the Great Solitude was first shown on PBS in May 1989 as part of the *Adventure* series.

Since then the film has been shown in England and other countries. It won second prize for profiles at the 1990 American Film Festival.

You can obtain *Into the Great Solitude* on VHS or Beta by writing or calling:

The New Film Company
7 Mystic Street, Suite 729
Arlington, MA 02174
(617) 641–2580